MW00916729

Daily Devotions for *Destiny*

365 Days of Discovering the Path to Your Destiny

Shirley McCleskey

WESTBOW
PRESS®
A DIVISION OF THOMAS NELSON
& ZONDERVAN

Scripture taken from the Amplified Bible, copyright © 1954, 1958, 1962, 1964, 1965, 1987 by The Lockman Foundation. Used by permission.

Scripture taken from the Holy Bible, NEW INTERNATIONAL VERSION®. Copyright © 1973, 1978, 1984, 2011 by Biblica, Inc. All rights reserved worldwide. Used by permission. NEW INTERNATIONAL VERSION® and NIV® are registered trademarks of Biblica, Inc. Use of either trademark for the offering of goods or services requires the prior written consent of Biblica US, Inc.

Scripture taken from The Living Bible copyright © 1971 by Tyndale House Foundation. Used by permission of Tyndale House Publishers Inc., Carol Stream, Illinois 60188. All rights reserved. The Living Bible, TLB, and the The Living Bible logo are registered trademarks of Tyndale House Publishers.

This book is a work of non-fiction. Unless otherwise noted, the author and the publisher make no explicit guarantees as to the accuracy of the information contained in this book and in some cases, names of people and places have been altered to protect their privacy.

WestBow Press books may be ordered through booksellers or by contacting:

WestBow Press
A Division of Thomas Nelson & Zondervan
1663 Liberty Drive
Bloomington, IN 47403
www.westbowpress.com
1 (866) 928-1240

Because of the dynamic nature of the Internet, any web addresses or links contained in this book may have changed since publication and may no longer be valid. The views expressed in this work are solely those of the author and do not necessarily reflect the views of the publisher, and the publisher hereby disclaims any responsibility for them.

Any people depicted in stock imagery provided by Getty Images are models, and such images are being used for illustrative purposes only. Certain stock imagery © Getty Images.

ISBN: 978-1-9736-4739-3 (sc)
ISBN: 978-1-9736-4738-6 (hc)
ISBN: 978-1-9736-4740-9 (e)

Library of Congress Control Number: 2018914262

Print information available on the last page.

WestBow Press rev. date: 12/26/2018

I Dedicate Daily Devotions for Destiny to my children, Jeremey and Jalisa. Jeremey, whose wisdom expands far beyond his years; has always been my rock and strength. He is a source of encouragement to me even when he needs encouragement himself. He is my greatest cheerleader and always has my back! Jalisa keeps me on my toes! She taught me the importance of not only knowing the scriptures but knowing the true meaning of the scriptures because if it does not sound right, she is going to challenge it! I am honored that God chose me to be your mom! Thank you both for being in my life and carrying on the legacy of Destiny!

January

"Before I formed you in the womb I knew you,
before you were born I set you apart;
I appointed you as a prophet to the nations."

Jeremiah 1:5 (NIV)

January 1

Daily Devotion for DESTINY:

Isaiah 43: 18-19 – (New International Version)

[18] Forget the former things; do not dwell on the past.

[19] See, I am doing a new thing! Now it springs up; do you not perceive it? I am making a way in the wilderness and streams in the wasteland.

Happy New Year! This is the beginning of a New Year and a new start for each one of us. I would like to spend this year learning how to use all the tools that God gave us to not only discover but walk out our individual destiny. Some of the tools that God has given us is meditation, transformation, wisdom, thankfulness and faith. Throughout the year, we will learn together how to apply each one of these tools in our lives.

I have watched many family and friends pass on without fulfilling their destiny and discovering their destiny. Some of them passed not even knowing that they had a specific assignment on this earth. Please join me on this year-long journey as we discover not only the reason for our existence, but how to walk it out.

II Corinthians 5:17; Isaiah 42:9; Revelation 21:5

January 2

Daily Devotion for DESTINY:

Jeremiah 29:10-11 (New International Version)

[10] This is what the LORD says: "When seventy years are completed for Babylon, I will come to you and fulfill my good promise to bring you back to this place.

[11] For I know the plans I have for you," declares the LORD, "plans to prosper you and not to harm you, plans to give you hope and a future.

This is God speaking to the exiles that he took from Jerusalem to Babylon at the end of 70 years of captivity. Do you feel like you have been held in captivity in your mind, will or emotions? Know that it is God's desire to bring you out of captivity in this season!

Many times, we do not know our own thoughts; nor our own mind. Know that God is never uncertain about His plan for our lives. Begin this new year by asking God about His plan for your life, then agree with Him when He begins to reveal His plans to you.

Isaiah 55:8; Psalms 33:11; Job 23:13

January 3

Daily Devotion for DESTINY:

Jeremiah 1:5 (New International Version)

"Before I formed you in the womb I knew[a] you, before you were born I set you apart; I appointed you as a prophet to the nations."

The moment that we were conceived, God gave us our assignment for our lives. Each one of us has a specific assignment and purpose that we are on this earth to accomplish. For Jeremiah, it was a Prophet to the nations.

What is your assignment? God is patiently waiting for us to ask this question of Him. If you do not already know what your purpose on this earth is, now is the perfect time to ask Him. He is waiting to reveal His desire for your life. Call unto Him and He will answer you!

Psalms 71:5-6; Galatians 1:15-16; Isaiah 44:2

January 4

Daily Devotion for DESTINY:

Jeremiah 29:12-14a (New International version)

[12] Then you will call on me and come and pray to me, and I will listen to you.

[13] You will seek me and find me when you seek me with all your heart.

[14] I will be found by you," declares the LORD, "and will bring you back from captivity.[a] I will gather you from all the nations and places where I have banished you," declares the LORD, "and will bring you back to the place from which I carried you into exile."

A very important part of seeking the Lord for your assignment in life is learning to hear his voice. When you go to God in prayer, it is a two-way conversation. Not only are you talking to Him, but He is speaking to you as well.

God cannot wait until you wake up in the morning to talk to you! If you speak with someone daily on your phone, you begin to know their voice as soon as they call. The same is true with God. Talk to Him as you would talk to your best friend (because He is) every day and you will begin to know His voice when He speaks to you.

Jeremiah 33:3; Isaiah 65:24; Luke 11:9-10

January 5

Daily Devotion for DESTINY:

Psalms 37:23 (The Amplified Bible)

The steps of a [good and righteous] man are directed and established by the Lord, and He delights in his way [and blesses his path].

Has your life gone off track? God is taking us back to the point where our lives went off track and giving us the opportunity to make better decisions that will allow us to get back on track. The decisions that we make from this point forward will determine our path.

Are we willing to leave some familiar things behind this time to go where God is trying to take us? Let's allow God to order our steps as we walk the path that He planned for us even before we were born!

Proverbs 16:9; Proverbs 4:26: Psalms 121:3

January 6

Daily Devotion for DESTINY:

Genesis 37:5-7 (New International Version)

[5] Joseph had a dream, and when he told it to his brothers, they hated him even more.

[6] He said to them, "Listen to this dream I had:

[7] We were binding sheaves of grain out in the field when suddenly my sheaf rose and stood upright, while your sheaves gathered around mine and bowed down to it."

I want to encourage everyone to hold on to their dreams and visions. Joseph was 17 years old when he had this dream. The scriptures go on to say that he had another dream where the sun, moon and stars bowed down to him. Because of these dreams, Joseph was hated by his brothers.

Because of the extreme hatred of his brothers, they decided to sell Joseph into slavery. Joseph was later thrown into jail (even though he was innocent) by Pharaoh. Throughout all these trials and tribulations, God was with him! Joseph realized that every struggle that he encountered was preparing him for his destiny.

Finally, in Genesis 42:6-7, Joseph (and his brothers) saw the dreams that he had at 17 years old manifest. Do not let the pain of holding on to your dreams and vision make you miss the joy of giving birth to them!

John 17:14; Genesis 42:9; Amos 3:7

January 7

Daily Devotion for DESTINY:

Psalms 139:14-16 (The Living Bible) – Thank you for making me so wonderfully complex! It is amazing to think about. Your workmanship is marvelous-and how well I know it.

You were there while I was being formed in utter seclusion! You saw me before I was born and scheduled each day of my life before I began to breathe. Every day was recorded in your book!

God made us unique which means that we have leverage. Nobody can be you and nobody can do what you can do. That is the advantage that God gave you! We must learn how to develop ourselves and capitalize on the advantage that God has given us.

It is vital to get into an atmosphere where you can grow to your maximum potential. Make it a point to seek out the individuals that God has ordained to speak to who you really are into your lives.

Most of us have not yet tapped into who we are totally. We have never really met ourselves in totality. It takes a lifetime to unpack all the genius that God put in you, so enjoy the journey of getting to know yourselves!

Genesis 1:26-27; Psalms 111:2; Psalms 40:5

January 8

Daily Devotion for DESTINY:

Matthew 11:28-30 (New International Version) – [28] "Come to me, all you who are weary and burdened, and I will give you rest. [29] Take my yoke upon you and learn from me, for I am gentle and humble in heart, and you will find rest for your souls. [30] For my yoke is easy and my burden is light."

Sometimes life will cause you to leak and this will cause a weariness in you. When you get weary, you get the wrong perspective. When you get weary, you cannot push your promise out. Wearied wombs will not deliver.

In this season, God is going to strengthen your womb. How do you get rid of weariness? Spend time talking to God and he will strengthen your womb. Get ready to give birth!

Isaiah 28:12; Romans 7:22-25; Galatians 5:1

January 9

Daily Devotion for DESTINY:

Mark 12:30 (The Amplified Bible, classic edition) - [30] And you shall love the Lord your God [a]out of *and* with your whole heart and out of *and* with all your soul (your [b]life) and out of *and* with all your mind (with [c]your faculty of thought and your moral understanding) and out of *and* with all your strength. [d]*This is the first and principal commandment.*

God wants us to love Him passionately. He wants to be constantly on our minds. If you have ever been in love, you understand that your desire is to please this person. When we set out to please God, He in return pleases us.

One of the ways to please God is to worship Him. The bible says in Psalms 150:6 (The Amplified Bible, Classic edition) [6] Let everything that has breath *and* every breath of life praise the Lord! Praise the Lord! (Hallelujah!)

Wherever your worship is, there will your heart be. Worship must be genuine. It must come from a heart that loves the Lord so much that your only desire is to please Him. Set out today to make God smile by giving Him your worship!

Revelation 4:11; Deuteronomy 6:5; Psalms 26:2

January 10

Daily Devotion for DESTINY:

Hebrews 12:1-2 (The New King James Version) - Therefore we also, since we are surrounded by so great a cloud of witnesses, let us lay aside every weight, and the sin which so easily ensnares *us,* and let us run with endurance the race that is set before us, ²looking unto Jesus, the author and finisher of *our* faith, who for the joy that was set before Him endured the cross, despising the shame, and has sat down at the right hand of the throne of God.

All of us are on a path in life. The people that have decided to follow their path to their destiny has become a target of satan. There is a reason that you are so stressed. There is a reason that you have been going through a season of drought. For some, it seems like a life-long drought.

The reason is because satan's job is to wear you down. He strategically tries to get you into relationships and circumstances that God never called you to be in and because it is too heavy to handle, it is wearing you out. There is no way to lay aside the weight without laying aside the stuff that is weighing you down.

Let this be the year that you lay aside the people and circumstances that are weighing you down so that you can run this race. We are surrounded by a great cloud of witnesses that are routing for us!

Luke 21:34; Colossians 3:5-8; II Corinthians 7:1

January 11

Daily Devotion for DESTINY:

I Peter 4:10 (The Living Bible) - God has given each of you some special abilities; be sure to use them to help each other, passing on to others God's many kinds of blessings.

We are all unique individuals. God created us with unique DNA. Even though God created us with our own unique DNA, He created us with everyone else in mind. What this means is that we are all connected. We are one piece of the puzzle in God's big picture.

Even though we have a unique assignment and a unique purpose, our purpose is connected to each other. What you do not have in you to fulfill your purpose is hidden in someone else. An English author by the name of John Donne said that "No man is an island unto himself." We need each other! God created it that way!

Make sure in this year that you watch for the divine connections that God is going to send you to help you fulfill your destiny!

Romans 15:1-3; Mark 10:45; Hebrews 6:10

January 12

Daily Devotion for DESTINY:

Philippians 4:7-8 (The Amplified Bible)- And the peace of God [that peace which reassures the heart, that peace] which transcends all understanding, [that peace which] stands guard over your hearts and your minds in Christ Jesus [is yours].8 Finally, [a]believers, whatever is true, whatever is honorable and worthy of respect, whatever is right and confirmed by God's word, whatever is pure and wholesome, whatever is lovely and brings peace, whatever is admirable and of good repute; if there is any excellence, if there is anything worthy of praise, think continually on these things [center your mind on them, and implant them in your heart].

The key to emerging from our current mindsets with our minds in tact is our ability to elevate our minds. Our mind is the command central of our bodies, so satan wishes to control our minds. When a thought enters your mind, it is transferred through your spirit and your body manifests it. The power of a thought is just as powerful as a physical manifestation.

Philippians 4:8 tells us how to think so that we can manifest the mind of Christ. Let us determine that this is the year that we perfect our thought life!

Romans 12:2; Proverbs 4:23; Colossians 3:2-5

January 13

Daily Devotion for DESTINY:

Genesis 8:22 (The Amplified Bible) - While the earth remains, Seedtime and harvest, Cold and heat, Winter and summer, and day and night Shall not cease."

So many people are dealing with frustration and anxiety. Many are frustrated with where they are in life because what they saw and perceived in their minds about their life has not yet manifested. They thought surely by now some things would have manifested.

Much of this frustration comes from not knowing what season in life you are in at this moment. If you discover what season in life you are in, it will give you the patience to wait for the manifestation of what you are believing God for.

In our scripture for today, God set a principle in motion. The principle is that as long as the earth remains, there will be seed…. time….harvest. When you plant a seed, you do not get a harvest right away. What happens between the planting of a seed and the harvest? **TIME!**

Take the time this year to discover what season you are in. If you are not yet in your harvest season, HOLD ON! You will be. No season lasts forever, so your harvest season is coming!

Ecclesiastes 3:1-8; Song of Solomon 2:11-12; Ecclesiastes 7:14

January 14

Daily Devotion for DESTINY:

Proverbs 4:23 (The Amplified Bible)- Watch over your heart with all diligence, for from it flow the springs of life.

Above everything else, we must guard the way we think and the way that we feel because life flows from our heart. We must learn how to guard our heart without mistreating people while still treating ourselves the way we should be treated.

The problem with a lot of people is that they are too influenced by other people's thoughts and feelings about them. We learned a few days ago that God sends people to speak into our lives. We want to welcome these people into our lives because they are there to help us get to our destiny.

satan also sends people into our lives. They are there to steal your joy, confidence, courage, peace, beliefs and most importantly; the positive thoughts that you have about yourself. These are the people that you want to guard your heart from. There are enough people that doubt your destiny; why join them?

James 1:14-15; Mark 14:38; Deuteronomy 4:9

January 15

Daily Devotion for DESTINY:

Genesis 6:13-17 – (New International Version) – [13] So God said to Noah, "I am going to put an end to all people, for the earth is filled with violence because of them. I am surely going to destroy both them and the earth. [14] So make yourself an ark of cypress[a] wood; make rooms in it and coat it with pitch inside and out. [15] This is how you are to build it: The ark is to be three hundred cubits long, fifty cubits wide and thirty cubits high.[b] [16] Make a roof for it, leaving below the roof an opening one cubit[c] high all around.[d] Put a door in the side of the ark and make lower, middle and upper decks. [17] I am going to bring floodwaters on the earth to destroy all life under the heavens, every creature that has the breath of life in it. Everything on earth will perish.

When God gave Noah the instructions to build an ark, there had never been rain let alone flood waters on the earth. It took great faith for Noah to follow the instructions of God concerning things that he had never seen.

Why do we need faith? Many times, whatever God says is usually not so at the time that He says it; therefore, He is looking for a people who have enough faith to believe what He says until it manifests itself.

God is trying to manifest His presence here on earth. He is looking for a people that will trust Him even when they can't trace Him! Determine in your heart that this is the year that you increase your faith in God!

Hebrews 11:6-7; Genesis 7:23; II Peter 3:6-7

January 16

Daily Devotion for DESTINY:

Philippians 3:13-14 (The Amplified Bible) - [13][a]Brothers and sisters, I do not consider that I have made it my own yet; but one thing *I do*: forgetting what *lies* behind and reaching forward to what *lies* ahead, [14]I press on toward the goal to win the [heavenly] prize of the upward call of God in Christ Jesus.

Ben Franklin once said, "Some People die at 25, but are not buried until 75. What this means that that they keep on existing, but they stop living. They concede to the difficulties in life. Many people quit living because they cannot get beyond their past. They cannot get beyond the circumstances that took them off track.

satan's job is to make us continue to focus on and feel the effects of our past so that we will not focus on and reach our destiny. We will only be able to get the things that God has in store for our future to the degree that we can forget the things that lie behind us.

Make this year the year that you forget the things that lie behind and press towards the great things that God has in store for you ahead!!!

Isaiah 43:18-19; Deuteronomy 8:2; Isaiah 65:17

January 17

Daily Devotion for DESTINY:

Matthew 6:10 (The Amplified Bible) – Your Kingdom come, Your will be done on earth as it is in heaven.

Are you tired of being ordinary? Are you tired of seeing status quo in your life? Are you ready for God to do something supernatural in your life? We are a people that was born in the image and likeness of God. What this means that that God has destined for us to live in an atmosphere that is conducive to our spirits.

God wants to make us witnesses of the possessing Heaven on earth. He wants us to be the supernatural beings that He created us to be so that when people see us, they see Him! God wants people to look at our lives and know that He is alive because only God could have done that!

You have been chosen to change your atmosphere. Let this year be the year that God shows you off!

Romans 8:19; Philippians 1:20; I John 3:2

January 18

Daily Devotion for DESTINY:

II Corinthians 5:17 (The Amplified Bible) - Therefore if anyone is in Christ [that is, grafted in, joined to Him by faith in Him as Savior], *he is* a new creature [reborn and renewed by the Holy Spirit]; the old things [the previous moral and spiritual condition] have passed away. Behold, new things have come [because spiritual awakening brings a new life].

When we are born again, we should be continually moving forward. Many people are revolving instead of evolving. If your life looks exactly like it did last year and the year before, you are revolving.

If you feel stuck, it is a sign that you have quit evolving. God created us in seed form; therefore, His intention is that we constantly grow and evolve into the beautiful creation that He had in mind when He created us.

Some of the frustration that we feel is because we sense that we are evolving and changing. It is alright to change! It is alright to become a new creature! Make this year the year that you begin to evolve into the person that God created you to be!

Job 17:19; Isaiah 43:18; Philippians 3:12

January 19

Daily Devotion for DESTINY:

II Samuel 9:1-3 (New International Version) – 9 David asked, "Is there anyone still left of the house of Saul to whom I can show kindness for Jonathan's sake?" ² Now there was a servant of Saul's household named Ziba. They summoned him to appear before David, and the king said to him, "Are you Ziba?" "At your service," he replied. ³ The king asked, "Is there no one still alive from the house of Saul to whom I can show God's kindness?" Ziba answered the king, "There is still a son of Jonathan; he is lame in both feet."

Do you feel that you have been shortchanged? Have you ever invested more than you got back? Have you ever put more into a relationship than you received? Have you ever supported everyone else's vision only to find out that there was noon there to support your vision? If so, you have been short changed.

All of us have some area in our lives where we have made a full investment and received a poor return. In our scripture today, Mephibosheth was Saul's grandson and heir to the throne. He was dropped as an infant by his nurse and left lame in both feet; therefore, he was unable to inherit the throne which was rightfully his. He was short changed!

Just because you have been short changed does not mean you will not survive! God has you on His mind. He has not forgotten what you did not get! This is the season (year) of restoration! God is going to give you double for all your trouble!

I Samuel 23:16-18; I Samuel 18:1-4; I Samuel 20:42

January 20

Daily Devotion for DESTINY:

Philippians 4:6-7 (New International Version) - Do not be anxious about anything, but in every situation, by prayer and petition, with thanksgiving, present your requests to God. ⁷And the peace of God, which transcends all understanding, will guard your hearts and your minds in Christ Jesus.

A couple of months back, I saw a meme that really blessed me, and I wanted to share it today. It simply said, "It's Handled......God"!

In the coming hours, days, months, weeks and years, may these two words be a source of strength for you as it has for me.

I Timothy 2:1-2; II Chronicles 7:14; Jeremiah 29:7

January 21

Daily Devotion for DESTINY:

Psalms 27:1-2 (New International Version) – The LORD is my light and my salvation—whom shall I fear? The LORD is the stronghold of my life— of whom shall I be afraid? [2]When the wicked advance against me to devour[a] me, it is my enemies and my foes who will stumble and fall.

This Psalm written by David lets me know what an honor it is to know Jesus as my Lord and Savior. It is a reflection of David on how his faith in the power of God brought him though his many tests and trials.

As you go through your day today, take time to reflect on some of the times that God fought your battles and gave you the victory. In the process, you will realize that He is still fighting your battles and still giving you the victory. Do not fear – God is with you!!!

Psalms 56:13; II Corinthians 4:6; I John 1:5

January 22

Daily Devotion for DESTINY:

John 3:16 (The Amplified Bible) - [16]"For God so [greatly] loved *and* dearly prized the world, that He [even] gave His [One and] [a]only begotten Son, so that whoever believes *and* trusts in Him [as Savior] shall not perish, but have eternal life.

As I woke up this morning, I felt an overwhelming presence of God's love. I began to think about how He loves us unconditionally.

Even if you were the only person on earth, He would have still given His only begotten son just for you! Let that marinate!

Romans 5:8; I John 4:9-10; Ephesians 2:4

January 23

Daily Devotion for DESTINY:

Genesis 1:3-5 (New International Version) - And God said, "Let there be light," and there was light. [4] God saw that the light was good, and he separated the light from the darkness. [5] God called the light "day," and the darkness he called "night." And there was evening, and there was morning—the first day.

God has given us the same creative ability to frame our world that He used to frame the world that we live in. The power to frame our world is in our tongues.

The words that we speak must come out of our spirit. They must change us before it can change our world; therefore, we must get the word of God in our spirits.

The way that we get the word of God in our spirits is not just reading it but meditating on it day and night. What are you speaking into your world?

Joshua 1:8; Psalms 19:14; Luke 11:28

January 24

Daily Devotion for DESTINY:

II Timothy 4:7-8 (New International Version) --[7]I have fought the good fight, I have finished the race, I have kept the faith. [8]Now there is in store for me the crown of righteousness, which the Lord, the righteous Judge, will award to me on that day—and not only to me, but also to all who have longed for his appearing.

The new year is a great time to start a new season and a new beginning and I encourage you to do so; however, I also encourage to finish the new beginning that you started last year and the year before.

It is time to finish the book that you began writing a few years ago or that business plan that you started and never completed. Many of us do not have time to miss the timing of God anymore. Many of us do not have enough faith or resources to start completely over. We only have enough to finish what we have started.

Each of us are running a different race, but we are all running the race to keep our faith. Our goal is to finish our race while fighting to keep the faith!

Acts 20:24; I Corinthians 9:24-26; I Timothy 6:12

January 25

Daily Devotion for DESTINY:

James 3:17 (The Amplified Bible) - [17]But the wisdom from above is first pure [morally and spiritually undefiled], then peace-loving [courteous, considerate], gentle, reasonable [and willing to listen], full of compassion and good fruits. It is unwavering, without [self-righteous] hypocrisy [and self-serving guile].

God's desire for us is harmonious relationships. There is certainly a place for defending the truth and there is a right and a wrong way for defending the truth. The following are a few pointers from Bishop Tudor Bismarck on using wisdom in our relationships:

*I must reduce my public words and comments

*I must increase my hearing and listening

*I do not need to comment on everything

*I do not need to express my opinion on everything

*I must weigh the words of people who speak

*I must think more than once before making a decision

James 1:5; Proverbs 12:15; Proverbs 3:13-18

January 26

Daily Devotion for DESTINY:

James 5:16 (The Amplified Bible -classic edition)-¹⁶Confess to one another therefore your faults (your slips, your false steps, your offenses, your sins) and pray [also] for one another, that you may be healed *and* restored [to a spiritual tone of mind and heart]. The earnest (heartfelt, continued) prayer of a righteous man makes tremendous power available [dynamic in its working].

The bible instructs us to pray for one another. It lets us know that earnest, heartful prayers of a man that has been made righteous by the blood of Jesus has tremendous power.

We can either construct (build up) or destruct (tear down) our brothers and sisters. It is God's desire that we choose to build each other up.

Psalms 34:15; I John 3:22; Genesis 20:17

January 27

Daily Devotion for DESTINY:

Ephesians 6:13 (New International Version)- ¹³ Therefore put on the full armor of God, so that when the day of evil comes, you may be able to stand your ground, and after you have done everything, to stand.

I woke up with this song by Donnie McClurkin in my spirit this morning. Meditate on this and be blessed!

What do you do
when you've done all you can
And it seems like it's never enough?
You just stand

Be not entangled in that bondage again
You just stand and be sure
God has a purpose
Yes, God has a plan

Psalms 119:89-91; I Corinthians 15:58; I Timothy 6:12

January 28

Daily Devotion for DESTINY:

I Peter 4:12-13 (New International Version) - [12]Dear friends, do not be surprised at the fiery ordeal that has come on you to test you, as though something strange were happening to you. [13]But rejoice in as much as you participate in the sufferings of Christ, so that you may be overjoyed when his glory is revealed.

The bible lets us know that in this Christian walk, we will encounter trials and tribulations. Our faith must be tested. The good news is that once our faith has gone through the refining process, we shall come out as pure gold!

James 1:3 helps us to understand that the trying of our faith develops patience. Are you asking the Lord for more patience? Get ready for your faith to be tried!

Make this year the year that you allow God to take you through the refining process so that you can experience the glory that is just around the corner!

Luke 21:19; Hebrews 6:12; I Peter 1:7

January 29

Daily Devotion for DESTINY:

Proverbs 18:19 (The Amplified Bible -classic edition) - ¹⁹A brother offended is harder to be won over than a strong city, and [their] contentions separate them like the bars of a castle.

It is very important in this season to guard our friendships and relationships carefully. We must do all in our power to avoid disagreements and offences. The ones that you cannot avoid, you must settle quickly. The scripture is telling us that once we offend our brother or sister, it is hard to win them over.

We must offer the truth in the spirit of love. If you have offended your brother or sister, it is your duty to be reconciled as quickly as possible. If you have been offended, it is our duty as a Christian to forgive (even if we have not been asked) and be reconciled.

Let's make this year the year that we perfect our love for our brothers and sisters! Love covers a multitude of sins!

Ephesians 4:3; James 3:18; I Peter 4:8

January 30

Daily Devotion for DESTINY:

Habakkuk 2:2-3 (New International Version) – [2] Then the LORD replied: "Write down the revelation and make it plain on tablets so that a herald[a] may run with it. [3] For the revelation awaits an appointed time; it speaks of the end and will not prove false. Though it linger, wait for it; it[b] will certainly come and will not delay.

The above scripture is a word that God gave to His Prophet; however, it is very relevant for your personal vision. It is important to write your dreams and visions down so that it can be read over and over again. We know that the faith that we have for our dreams and visions will be tested, so it is important to remember in the dark what God said to you in the light!

God lets us know that our vision will be delayed. Many times, this is because He must prepare us for our vision and our dreams. He also lets us know that it will come so do not give up on the vision that God has given you. Determine to go through the process so that you can see it come to pass!

Psalms 27:14; Hebrews 10:36-37; James 5:7-8

January 31

Daily Devotion for DESTINY:

I Peter 5:10 (The Amplified Bible – classic edition) - [10]And after you have suffered a little while, the God of all grace [Who imparts all blessing and favor], Who has called you to His [own] eternal glory in Christ *Jesus*, will Himself complete *and* make you what you ought to be, establish *and* ground you securely, and strengthen, and settle you.

It is the things that we go through that makes us who we are. For everyone that is trying not to go through, you are delaying your destiny. Go ahead and go through! One songwriter said that there is a blessing on the other side of through!

Make this year the year that you allow Jesus to establish, ground, settle, strengthen and complete you!

James 1:12; Romans 12:12; St. John 16:33

February

For I know the plans I have for you," declares the Lord,
"plans to prosper you and not to harm you,
plans to give you hope and a future.
Jeremiah 29:11 (NIV)

February 1

Daily Devotion for DESTINY:

Psalms 37:3-4 (The Amplified Bible -classic edition) - ³Trust (lean on, rely on, and be confident) in the Lord and do good; so shall you dwell in the land and feed surely on His faithfulness, *and* truly you shall be fed.⁴Delight yourself also in the Lord, and He will give you the desires *and* secret petitions of your heart.

If we get the wisdom of this scripture, we will find ourselves living out our destiny and enjoying the journey. Many people only see the part of the scripture that says that God will give you the desires and petitions of your heart.

Over the years, I have learned that this is totally true! For the scripture to work, you must trust in the Lord and delight yourself in Him. As you truly trust Him and delight yourself in Him, you will find that your desires and the secret petitions of your heart begin to change to His desires for you. He will certainly fulfill His desires for your life.

Let's purpose in our hearts to make this year the year that we delight ourselves in the Lord and only desire His will for us!

John 15:7; Job 22:26; I John 5:14-15

February 2

Daily Devotion for DESTINY:

I Peter 5:7 (The Amplified Bible-classic edition) - **7**Casting the [a] whole of your care [all your anxieties, all your worries, all your concerns, [b]once and for all] on Him, for He cares for you affectionately *and* cares about you watchfully.

When you are under pressure from worry, tell God about it and let Him help you deal with it. Our bodies were not designed to worry and to be anxious. One of the greatest purposes of our lives is to be transformed into His image and likeness. Unfortunately, one of the ways we are transformed is through trials and tribulations and how we handle them.

Decide today to trade your fears, worries and cares for God's peace and rest in Him!

Psalms 34:17-18; Matthew 11:28; Isaiah 41:10

February 3

Daily Devotion for DESTINY:

Jeremiah 32:27 (The Amplified Bible - classic edition) - 27 Behold, I am the Lord, the God of all flesh; is there anything too hard for Me?

One of the things that gives me great pleasure as a believer is that I serve a God of assurance. He knows our end from our beginning. He knows what we need even before we ask.

When you don't know what to do, God knows what to do. When people say that you can't, God says that you can because there is nothing too hard for Him; therefore, there is nothing too hard for you because you belong to Him!

Matthew 19:26; Jeremiah 32:17; Genesis 18:14

February 4

Daily Devotion for DESTINY:

Joshua 5:6 (The Amplified Bible - classic edition) - 6 For the Israelites walked forty years in the wilderness till all who were men of war who came out of Egypt perished, because they did not hearken to the voice of the Lord; to them the Lord swore that He would not let them see the land which the Lord swore to their fathers to give us, a land flowing with milk and honey.

Like the Israelites, we as Christians are between the promise and the fulfillment of the promise. As a Christian, how are we handling our wilderness? Most scholars say that the journey that the Israelites were on was only an 11-day journey.

They "turned back" when the road looked difficult ahead. They failed to obey God's instructions. They did not trust God and His plan for them. Still, God was with them and they lacked nothing!

Let's make this year the year that we end our wilderness journey and enter our Promise land!

Deuteronomy 2:7; Psalms 95:10-11; Jeremiah 2:2

February 5

Daily Devotion for DESTINY:

II Corinthians 10:3-4 (The Amplified Bible - classic edition) - 3 For though we walk (live) in the flesh, we are not carrying on our warfare according to the flesh and using mere human weapons.

4 For the weapons of our warfare are not physical [weapons of flesh and blood], but they are mighty before God for the overthrow and destruction of strongholds.

Even though we are in the flesh, the above scripture lets us know that our struggles are not fleshly struggles, but spiritual struggles. The following are a few suggestions to shorten your struggles:

- Monitor your speaking - words create an environment for change!

- Yield - Surrender your will to God's will!

- Sing - Singing breaks the chains of oppression!

- Gain knowledge - Knowledge creates opportunity!

- Learn the lesson - So that you can be promoted!

Genesis 3:7-11; Exodus 32:25; Revelation 3:18

February 6

Daily Devotion for DESTINY:

II Peter 3:18 (The Amplified Bible) -18 but grow [spiritually mature] in the grace and knowledge of our Lord and Savior Jesus Christ. To Him be glory (honor, majesty, splendor), both now and to the day of eternity. Amen.

Did you know that God desire for us is that we constantly grow? Did you know that you can being a Christian does not guarantee growth? In our scripture for today, Peter instructs us to continue to grow in the grace and knowledge of our savior, Jesus Christ. This lets us know that growth is a continual process. It takes time.

Let's declare that this year will be the year that we grow in God on purpose!

Hebrews 5:12-13; I Timothy 4:7; II Timothy 3:16-17

February 7

Daily Devotion for DESTINY:

Galatians 4:19 (The Amplified Bible) - 19 My little children, for whom I am again in [the pains of] labor until Christ is [completely and permanently] formed within you—

Paul lets us know in our scripture for today that Christ must be formed in us. What this means is that once we accept Jesus in our lives, we must go through the process to become like Christ.

John Maxwell said it so well when he said, "We can teach what we know, but we reproduce what we are!" God's desire for us as Christians is that we reproduce other Christians. We do this by allowing Christ to be completely and permanently formed in us and then we can reproduce what we have become.

Romans 8:29; Philippians 1:8; Luke 22:44

February 8

Daily Devotion for DESTINY:

Proverbs 4:20-22 (The Amplified Bible-classic edition)- 20 My son, attend to my words; consent and submit to my sayings 21 Let them not depart from your sight; keep them in the center of your heart.22 For they are life to those who find them, healing and health to all their flesh.

Are you sick today? God's word has the directions for your healing. If you follow the medication plan that God has prescribed, it will bring life to your spirit, soul and body.

Let's honor God by taking His medicine, the word of God each and every day. When we are diligent to take our prescription, we will walk in total health!

Isaiah 55:3; Proverbs 6:20-21; Proverbs 12:18

February 9

Daily Devotion for DESTINY:

II Kings 6:15-16 (The Amplified Bible -classic edition) - When the servant of the man of God rose early and went out, behold, an army with horses and chariots was around the city. Elisha's servant said to him, Alas, my master! What shall we do?16 [Elisha] answered, Fear not; for those with us are more than those with them.

This scripture is a good representation of God's provision for us. When we feel that we are fighting our battles all by ourselves, God lets us know that He is fighting with us and with Him on our side, we are the majority!

There are two things that we need to appropriate God's provision for us. They are insight and trust in Him. Let God roll back the heavens and show you the host of Angels that are fighting on your behalf! You got this!!!

Isaiah 41:10-14; Romans 8:31; Psalms 55:18

February 10

Daily Devotion for DESTINY:

Hebrews 11:6 (The Living Bible) - 6 You can never please God without faith, without depending on him. Anyone who wants to come to God must believe that there is a God and that he rewards those who sincerely look for him.

This is Faith Day, so I would like to emphasize the importance of having faith in God. The scripture tells us that it is impossible to please God without faith. We must believe that He is who He says He is and that He loves us like He says He does.

The greatest reward you can have when you are seeking something is to find it. When we seek God, He rewards us by revealing Himself to us and through us. God is not trying to play Hide-n-go seek! His desire is that we find Him.

Let's make this year the year that we seek God as never before and watch Him reveal Himself to us in a different way each day!

Jeremiah 29:13-14; Proverbs 8:17; Matthew 6:33

February 11

Daily Devotion for DESTINY:

Matthew 13:3-8 (The Living Bible) - "A farmer was sowing grain in his fields. 4 As he scattered the seed across the ground, some fell beside a path, and the birds came and ate it. 5 And some fell on rocky soil where there was little depth of earth; the plants sprang up quickly enough in the shallow soil, 6 but the hot sun soon scorched them, and they withered and died, for they had so little root. 7 Other seeds fell among thorns, and the thorns choked out the tender blades. 8 But some fell on good soil and produced a crop that was thirty, sixty, and even a hundred times as much as he had planted.

Jesus' disciples asked him why He always used hard-to-understand illustrations after He taught the parable of the Sower. The message from this parable is so important that Matthew, Mark and Luke recorded it in their gospels. It is an honor and privilege to have insight into the Kingdom of Heaven (God's way of doing things). Jesus said that not everyone has been given this insight.

As we hear the word of God preached or read the word of God for ourselves, we must allow God to reveal to us what that word means for us as individuals and how we should apply it to our lives.

Let's make this year the year that we become that GOOD SOIL that Jesus spoke about in His parable and produce 30, 60 or better yet 100-fold return for the Kingdom!

Luke 8:10; Mark 4:11-12; John 16:25

February 12

Daily Devotion for DESTINY:

I Corinthians 13:1-10 (The Living Bible) - **13**If I had the gift of being able to speak in other languages without learning them and could speak in every language there is in all of heaven and earth, but didn't love others, I would only be making noise. **2**If I had the gift of prophecy and knew all about what is going to happen in the future, knew everything about *everything,* but didn't love others, what good would it do? Even if I had the gift of faith so that I could speak to a mountain and make it move, I would still be worth nothing at all without love. **3**If I gave everything I have to poor people, and if I were burned alive for preaching the Gospel but didn't love others, it would be of no value whatever.

4Love is very patient and kind, never jealous or envious, never boastful or proud, **5**never haughty or selfish or rude. Love does not demand its own way. It is not irritable or touchy. It does not hold grudges and will hardly even notice when others do it wrong. **6**It is never glad about injustice but rejoices whenever truth wins out. **7**If you love someone, you will be loyal to him no matter what the cost. You will always believe in him, always expect the best of him, and always stand your ground in defending him.

8All the special gifts and powers from God will someday come to an end, but love goes on forever. Someday prophecy and speaking in unknown languages and special knowledge—these gifts will disappear. **9**Now we know so little, even with our special gifts, and the preaching of those most gifted is still so poor. **10**But when we have been made perfect and complete, then the need for these inadequate special gifts will come to an end, and they will disappear.

Now, let's let that marinate!!!

I Peter 4:8; I Timothy 1:5; Galatians 5:22

February 13

Daily Devotion for DESTINY:

Psalms 1:1-2 (The Amplified Bible- classic edition) -**1** Blessed (happy, fortunate, prosperous, and enviable) is the man who walks *and* lives not in the counsel of the unGodly [following their advice, their plans and purposes], nor stands [submissive and inactive] in the path where sinners walk, nor sits down [to relax and rest] where the scornful [and the mockers] gather.

2 But his delight *and* desire are in the law of the Lord, and on His law (the precepts, the instructions, the teachings of God) he habitually meditates (ponders and studies) by day and by night.

Today is Meditation Day! Biblical Meditation means reflective thinking about spiritual truths. While you are meditating (pondering) on the Word of God, you are allowing God to speak to your spirit about His word.

We are to study the scriptures, but for our study to be effective, we must also develop the art of meditation. Let this year be our year to not only study the scriptures but meditate on them.

Joshua 1:8; Isaiah 55:8-9; Psalms 143:5

February 14

Daily Devotion for DESTINY:

Romans 12:2 (The Amplified Bible, classic edition) - **2** Do not be conformed to this world (this age), [fashioned after and adapted to its external, superficial customs], but be transformed (changed) by the [entire] renewal of your mind [by its new ideals and its new attitude], so that you may prove [for yourselves] what is the good and acceptable and perfect will of God, *even* the thing which is good and acceptable and perfect [in His sight for you].

It's Transformation Day! This is a great day to meditate on transforming our minds. True transformation takes place from the inside out. Our actions are a result of what we think and that is why it is important to transform our minds by studying and meditating on the Word of God.

We want to please God by walking in His will for our lives, so let's start today by letting God remove the things that cannot go through the transformation process with us!

II Corinthians 5:17; Ephesians 4:22-24; Colossians 3:10

February 15

Daily Devotion for DESTINY:

I Kings 3:9-12 (The Amplified Bible, classic edition) - **9** So give Your servant an understanding mind *and* a hearing heart to judge Your people, that I may discern between good and bad. For who is able to judge *and* rule this Your great people? **10** It pleased the Lord that Solomon had asked this. **11** God said to him, because you have asked this and have not asked for long life or for riches, nor for the lives of your enemies, but have asked for yourself understanding to recognize what is just and right, **12** Behold, I have done as you asked. I have given you a wise, discerning mind, so that no one before you was your equal, nor shall any arise after you equal to you.

Welcome to Wisdom Day! Today, I want to talk about the importance and benefits of Wisdom. King Solomon was the wisest man that ever lived. In the above scripture, the Lord asked the King what He can give him. Instead of asking for riches and many other fleshly things that he could have asked, the King asked for wisdom to lead God's people. You may not be a King, but wisdom is still a necessary attribute for each of us as we interact with people.

Because God was pleased with this request from King Solomon, He not only bestowed wisdom upon him, but God gave the King all the riches, health and the other things that he did not ask for.

We could learn a great lesson from King Solomon on the importance of having wisdom in our lives. Let's make this year the year that we grow in wisdom!

James 1:5; Proverbs 16:6; Psalms 119:34

February 16

Daily Devotion for DESTINY:

Psalms 136:1 (The Amplified Bible, classic edition) -**1** O give thanks to the Lord, for He is good; for His mercy *and* loving-kindness endure forever.

It is Thankful Day! Let us give thanks to God today just because He is good! Feel free to post why you are thankful to God in the comments and allow your brothers and sisters to rejoice with you!

Let' decide that this will be the year that we elevate our thankfulness to Father God! After all, He is a good, good Father!

II Chronicles 20:21; Ezra 3:11; II Chronicles 7:6

February 17

Daily Devotion for DESTINY:

Hebrews 11:1 (The Amplified Bible, classic edition) - **11** Now faith is the assurance (the confirmation, [a]the title deed) of the things [we] hope for, being the proof of things [we] do not see *and* the conviction of their reality [faith perceiving as real fact what is not revealed to the senses].

Happy Faith Day! Our scripture for today is the biblical definition of faith. Simply put, faith is believing God is who He says He is and that He will do what He says He will do!

As a parent, I know how I would feel if my children did not believe me and did not trust my word. I can imagine that is how Father God feels when we don't believe Him and trust his word. We learned that it is impossible to please God without faith (believing what He says).

Romans 12:3 tells us that God has distributed a measure of faith to each and every one of us. Let's make this year the year that we increase the faith that God has given us!

II Corinthians 5:7; Psalms 42:11; Titus 1:1

February 18

Daily Devotion for DESTINY:

Matthew 4:1 (The Amplified Bible, classic edition) -4 Then Jesus was led (guided) by the [Holy] Spirit into the wilderness (desert) to be tempted (tested and tried) by the devil.

There is one experience that all believers have in common. It has been dubbed "The Wilderness Experience". The wilderness is the part of life's journey where we experience temptations, hurts, disappointments, sickness and failures.

If Jesus was led into the wilderness to be tempted of satan, you can rest assured that we (the believers) will be as well. There is a purpose for the wilderness. It teaches us to depend on the Word of God to fight our battles, It helps the people in your world to get to know God as you know Him, It motivates us to do God's will and most importantly, the wilderness prepares us for our purpose so that we will reach our destiny!

Are you in the wilderness today? Rest assured that if you press forward using the example that Jesus set for us in the above scripture, you will come out victoriously just as He did!

Deuteronomy 8:2; Hebrews 2:18; Luke 4:1-13

February 19

Daily Devotion for DESTINY:

Romans 15:1-3 (God's Word Translation) - **15** So those of us who have a strong faith must be patient with the weaknesses of those whose faith is not so strong. We must not think only of ourselves. **2** We should all be concerned about our neighbor and the good things that will build his faith. **3** Christ did not think only of himself. Rather, as Scripture says, "The insults of those who insult you have fallen on me."

We have a responsibility as believers to encourage and build up our brothers and sisters if they are struggling in certain areas of their lives. We should not look to our own interest in these cases, but rather the interest of Christ and focus on building the Kingdom of God.

It is important for us to endure the struggles of our brothers and sisters without passing judgement, but rather strive to help them build their faith until they become strong in the areas that they once struggled in.

In Genesis 4:9, the Lord asked Cain, where is Abel your brother? Cain responded with the question, Am I my brother's keeper? This is after he killed his brother. I am here to declare that YES, we are our brother's keeper. Let's not kill each other with our tongues but let us make this year the year that we build each other up!!!

Galatians 6:1-2; I Corinthians 9:22; Romans 14:

February 20

Daily Devotion for DESTINY:

Psalms 139:1-5 (The Living Bible) - **139** O Lord, you have examined my heart and know everything about me. **2** You know when I sit or stand. When far away you know my every thought. **3** You chart the path ahead of me and tell me where to stop and rest. Every moment you know where I am. **4** You know what I am going to say before I even say it. **5** You both precede and follow me and place your hand of blessing on my head.

On this Meditation Day, I would like for you to meditate on the fact that God CHOSE you! I heard someone say that "People will count you out over rumors, but God chose you knowing all of the facts!"

The above scripture lets us know that God knows everything about us. Even with this information, He has chosen us and trusts us to discover our purpose and walk out our destiny. In doing so, you will affect not only the people in your world, but also the atmosphere around you. There are people counting on you to do what God has chosen you to do.

Let's make this year the year that we not only discover our destination but walk it out!

Jeremiah 1:5; Ephesians 2:10; Isaiah 46:10

February 21

Daily Devotion for DESTINY:

Isaiah 26:3 (The Amplified Bible, classic edition)- **3** You will guard him *and* keep him in perfect *and* constant peace whose mind [both its inclination and its character] is stayed on You, because he commits himself to You, leans on You, *and* hopes confidently in You.

Today is Transformation Day and we are in the process of transforming our minds and our thoughts. This is very important because it is with the mind that we serve the Lord. The mind is the command central of our bodies. Our thoughts turn into actions; therefore, we must transform our thoughts.

The above scripture lets us know that God will give us constant peace if we keep our minds focused on Him. Let's make this year the year that we stay focused on the things of God. Do not let distractions interrupt your peace!

Philippians 4:6-7; John 14:27; Romans 5:1

February 22

Daily Devotion for DESTINY:

James 3:17 (The Amplified Bible, classic edition) - **17** But the wisdom from above is first of all pure (undefiled); then it is peace-loving, courteous (considerate, gentle). [It is willing to] yield to reason, full of compassion and good fruits; it is wholehearted *and* straightforward, impartial *and* unfeigned (free from doubts, wavering, and insincerity).

On this Wisdom Day, our scripture explains to us what the wisdom of God looks like. Earlier in the scripture it explains what the wisdom of the world looks like. Our goal is to have the wisdom of God.

God's wisdom has fruit! Its character has heavenly attributes and not selfish worldly attributes. Do you want this wisdom that comes from God? James 1:5 lets us know that if we lack wisdom, we just need to ask God for it. It is God's gift and all we have to do is receive it from Him.

I Corinthians 2:6-7; James 1:5; Luke 21:15

February 23

Daily Devotion for DESTINY:

Psalms 34:1-3 (New International Version) -
I will extol the LORD at all times;
his praise will always be on my lips.
²I will glory in the LORD;
let the afflicted hear and rejoice.
³Glorify the LORD with me;
let us exalt his name together.

On this Thankful Day, I would like to the Lord for my life, health and strength. I thank God for Jesus who died for me because He first loved me. I thank the Lord for the activity of all of my limbs. We don't realize how important it is to have the activity of all of your limbs until you lose the activity of a few. I thank God that I walk in uncommon favor in every area of my life!

I thank God that I am His sheep and I do hear, know and obey His voice. Even in the times when He says go right and I go left, He gently nudges me back on the path that He destined for me! I thank the Lord for the angels that encamp about me, my children and everyone that is connected to me to keep us safe from dangers seen and unseen! I thank God that no weapon formed against me will prosper and every tongue that rise up against me, God will condemn!

What are you thankful for today?

I Thessalonians 5:18; Ephesians 5:20; Acts 16:25

February 24

Daily Devotion for Destiny:

II Corinthians 5:7 (The Amplified Bible, classic edition) - **7** For we walk by faith [we [b]regulate our lives and conduct ourselves by our conviction or belief respecting man's relationship to God and divine things, with trust and holy fervor; thus we walk] not by sight *or* appearance.

Good morning and happy Faith Day! Man says, "Seeing is believing", so when we see something that becomes our truth. Our scripture today is challenging the believer to rise above what we see in the natural and live our lives based upon our faith and our trust in God and His word.

Let's determine to make this year the year that we live our lives according to what God says rather than what our circumstances say. Today is the perfect day to start the process!

Romans 8:24-25; I Peter 1:8; Hebrews 10:38

February 25

Daily Devotion for DESTINY:

Matthew 5:9 (The Amplified Bible, classic edition) - **9** Blessed (enjoying [a]enviable happiness, [b]spiritually prosperous—[c]with life-joy and satisfaction in God's favor and salvation, regardless of their outward conditions) are the makers *and* [d] maintainers of peace, for they shall be called the sons of God!

Sons of God has the character of their Father. I Thessalonians 5:23 tells us that our God is a God of peace. God is not only a peace-loving God, but He is also a peacemaking God. Just to clarify, the "peace at any price" mentality is not what God had in mind.

A person that ignores the problem acting as if everything is alright when it is not is not a peacemaker. We must use the wisdom of God to address problems while still keeping peace.

Let's begin this year learning how to be a peacemaker and not a preacebreaker!

Romans 16:20; I Thessalonians 5:23; Hebrews 13:20

February 26

Daily Devotion for DESTINY:

II Corinthians 10:3-4 (New International Version)- [3] For though we live in the world, we do not wage war as the world does. [4] The weapons we fight with are not the weapons of the world. On the contrary, they have divine power to demolish strongholds.

Every Christian's life is a warfare with satan. The battle that we fight with satan is in our minds. I Timothy 6:12 tells us to fight the good fight of Faith. satan's goal is to cause us to lose our Faith in God and in our destiny.

We must fight this mind battle by meditating on the word of God, transforming our minds, seeking God's wisdom, thanking God for where He has brought us from and where He is taking us to and most of all, developing our Faith. Let's make this year the year that we upgrade our weapons and win this fight!

I Timothy 1:18; Ephesians 6:13-18; Joshua 6:20

February 27

Daily Devotion for DESTINY:

Philippians 4:8 (The Living Bible) - **8** And now, brothers, as I close this letter, let me say this one more thing: Fix your thoughts on what is true and good and right. Think about things that are pure and lovely, and dwell on the fine, good things in others. Think about all you can praise God for and be glad about.

Happy Meditation Day! Today we are going to meditate on the things that will give us a healthy thought life. We have learned that our thoughts from the basis of our behavior; therefore, a Godly thought life is essential for a victorious Christian walk.

We are revisiting this scripture today because it reminds us what things we should meditate on to form a healthy thought life. Let this be the year that we become intentional about forming and maintaining Godly thoughts.

II Peter 1:3-7; II Corinthians 8:21; I Thessalonians 5:21-22

February 28

Daily Devotion for DESTINY:

Ezekiel 36:26 (The Living Bible) - **26** And I will give you a new heart—I will give you new and right desires—and put a new spirit within you. I will take out your stony hearts of sin and give you new hearts of love.[a]

Good morning and welcome to Transformation Day! Today, our scripture talks about a transformed heart and renewed spirit. Our heart is where our affections lie, where our desires are formed and where our reasoning takes place.

The greatest commandment according to Jesus in Matthew 22:37 is that we Love the Lord our God with all of our heart. The bible goes on to tell us in John 14:15 that if we love the Lord, we will keep His commandments. It takes a transformed heart to love God to the point that we keep His commandments

Let's decide that this is the year that we allow God to transform our hearts of stone into hearts of flesh that is capable of loving Him as well as our brothers and sisters.

Ezekiel 11:19-20; Psalms 51:10; Deuteronomy 30:6

March

For the revelation awaits an appointed time;
it speaks of the end
and will not prove false.
Though it lingers, wait for it;
it[a] will certainly come
and will not delay.

Habakkuk 2:3 (NIV)

March 1

Daily Devotion for DESTINY:

Proverbs 13:20 (The Amplified Bible) - He who walks [as a companion] with wise men will be wise, But the companions of [conceited, dull-witted] fools [are fools themselves and] will experience harm.

Welcome to Wisdom Day! Our scripture today helps us to understand the importance of who we hang out with. You can generally identify someone by the company that they keep. We tend to hang out with people whose spirit is like our own. Hence, the saying "Birds of a feather flock together."

On this Wisdom Day, let's choose to hang out with the wise and draw from their wisdom. Haven't we spent enough time hanging out with the unwise (or fools according to the scripture).

This year, allow God to lead you to the divine connections that He has planned for you so that they can impart the wisdom that you need to get to your destination!

I Corinthians 15:33-34; Proverbs 15:31; Acts 2:42

March 2

Daily Devotion for DESTINY:

Psalms 100: 1-5 (The Amplified Bible, classic edition) - **1** Make a joyful noise to the Lord, all you lands! **2** Serve the Lord with gladness! Come before His presence with singing!

3 Know (perceive, recognize, and understand with approval) that the Lord is God! It is He Who has made us, not we ourselves [and we are His]! We are His people and the sheep of His pasture. **4** Enter into His gates with thanksgiving *and* a thank offering and into His courts with praise! Be thankful *and* say so to Him, bless *and* affectionately praise His name!**5** For the Lord is good; His mercy *and* loving-kindness are everlasting; His faithfulness *and* truth endure to all generations.

It is Thankful Day! The normal response of a thankful heart is praise and worship. We are encouraged to worship God cheerfully. The motive of our worship is very important. We must know not only who God is, but who He is to us!

Today, let's not ask God for anything, but thank Him for all of the things that He has already done.

Isaiah 42:10-12; Romans 15:10; Zephaniah 3:14

March 3

Daily Devotion for DESTINY:

Mark 11:22-24 (The Amplified Bible, classic edition) -**2** And Jesus, replying, said to them, Have faith in God [constantly].**23** Truly I tell you, whoever says to this mountain, Be lifted up and thrown into the sea! and does not doubt at all in his heart but believes that what he says will take place, it will be done for him.**24** For this reason I am telling you, whatever you ask for in prayer, believe (trust and be confident) that it is granted to you, and you will [get it].

Happy Faith Day! Our faith scripture today takes place in the middle of a conversation that Jesus was having with His disciples. A few days prior to this conversation, Jesus was hungry and saw a fig tree that appeared to have figs on it. On a fig tree, the fruit appears at the same time as the leaves. When He approached the tree to eat the figs, it had nothing but leaves. Even though it was not the season for the tree to have figs on it, the tree appeared have fruit (another sermon for another day!!).

At that time, Jesus cursed the fig tree and He and his disciples went about their business. The next day, they passed by the tree and one of the disciples (Peter) noticed that the tree had withered away! Jesus took this teaching opportunity to let His disciples know that if we have faith in God and do not doubt in our hearts, we will have the same results.

This year, let's grow our faith by hearing, meditating on and speaking the word of God!

Matthew 21:22; I John 5:14-15; John 15:17

March 4

Daily Devotion for DESTINY:

Daniel 3: 24-25 (New International Version) - **24** Then King Nebuchadnezzar leaped to his feet in amazement and asked his advisers, "Weren't there three men that we tied up and threw into the fire? "They replied, "Certainly, Your Majesty."**25** He said, "Look! I see four men walking around in the fire, unbound and unharmed, and the fourth looks like a son of the Gods."

Our scripture today is about three Hebrew boys who lived righteous lives, yet they literally had to endure a fiery trial. Their king built a golden image and commanded everyone to worship the image at his command. The three Hebrews boys refused to worship the image because they worshipped the one and only true and living God.

They were thrown in the fire. When the king checked on them expecting them to be consumed by the fire, he found that not only were they not consumed, but God was in the midst of the fire with them.

The scripture goes on to say that their hair was not singed, their clothes was not burned and they didn't even smell like smoke! Hallelujah! This caused the king to praise the God of the three Hebrew boys and he promoted them in Babylon.

You can rest assured that as believers, we are going to go through some fiery trials, but know that you are not alone. God is with you. Allow God to deliver you and watch the Kingdom grow. After all, who wouldn't serve a God like this?

Isaiah 43:1-2; Daniel 3:22; Daniel 3:9-10

March 5

Daily Devotion for DESTINY:

Habakkuk 2:2-3 (The Amplified Bible, classic edition) - **2** And the Lord answered me and said, Write the vision and engrave it so plainly upon tablets that everyone who passes may [be able to] read [it easily and quickly] as he hastens by.**3** For the vision is yet for an appointed time and it hastens to the end [fulfillment]; it will not deceive *or* disappoint. Though it tarry, wait [earnestly] for it, because it will surely come; it will not be behindhand on its appointed day.

I wanted to revisit the above scriptures today and go a little more in depth about the importance of birthing the vision that God has given you. The first step in accomplishing the vision is to bring the vision from your spirit into the natural realm. You do this by writing it down.

Vision gives pain a purpose. We must be very careful that we do not get so preoccupied with the pain of holding on to our vision that we miss the joy of giving birth to it. Sometimes, we want to take the path of least resistance to try to avoid pain.

Let us make up in our minds that this is the year that we are going to write down our vision, hold on to it and watch God bring it to pass!

Hebrews 10:36-37; Daniel 8:19; Isaiah 30:18

March 6

Daily Devotion for DESTINY:

Matthew 7:17-20 (The Living Bible) - **7** Different kinds of fruit trees can quickly be identified by examining their fruit. **18** A variety that produces delicious fruit never produces an inedible kind. And a tree producing an inedible kind can't produce what is good. **19** So the trees having the inedible fruit are chopped down and thrown on the fire. **20** Yes, the way to identify a tree or a person[a] is by the kind of fruit produced.

It is Meditation Day! Our devotion a few days ago was about having faith to cause the fruitless areas in our lives to die by speaking to them. today, I wanted to expound on the tree that Jesus cursed because it had leaves which normally means that it had fruit as well.

Jesus was hungry, so He approached the tree to eat the fruit that should have been there and He found nothing but leaves. Let us make sure that our brothers and sisters that are hungry for Christ finds fruit when they approach us and not just leaves.

What are leaves? They are the scriptures that we post on Facebook, Instagram and Twitter. What is fruit? It is our life that is in line with the scriptures that we post.

Let us meditate on Galatians 5:22-23. These scriptures spell out the fruit that we display when the Holy Spirit is present within us. It will help us line our lives up with the Word of God!

James 1:22; Romans 2:13; Luke 11:28

March 7

Daily Devotion for DESTINY:

II Corinthians 5:17 (The Amplified Bible, classic edition) -**17** Therefore if any person is [engrafted] in Christ (the Messiah) he is a new creation (a new creature altogether); the old [previous moral and spiritual condition] has passed away. Behold, the fresh *and* new has come!

Good morning! It is Transformation Day! Transformation means to change from a life that conforms to the world's way of doing things to doing things God's way. The process of transformation begins once we accept Jesus as our Lord and Savior. At this time, we begin to transform our minds by reading God's word and becoming familiar with His way of doing things.

Evidence of transformation within us is seen as we begin to look more and more like our Father, God. We begin to take on His character and His personality.

Let's make this the year that we transform our lives by reading God's word and becoming familiar with His way of thinking and His way of doing things.

Ezekiel 36:26; Isaiah 43:18-19; Romans 6:4-6

March 8

Daily Devotion for DESTINY:

Colossians 1:9 (The Amplified Bible, classic edition) -**9** For this reason we also, from the day we heard of it, have not ceased to pray *and* make [[a]special] request for you, [asking] that you may be filled with the [b] full (deep and clear) knowledge of His will in all spiritual wisdom [[c]in comprehensive insight into the ways and purposes of God] understanding *and* discerning spiritual things.

Happy Wisdom Day! The scriptures tell us in Proverbs 9:10 that the fear of the Lord is the beginning of wisdom and the knowledge of the Holy One is insight and understanding. Wisdom and knowledge go hand in hand. Wisdom begins with reverence and respect for God's word and His desire for our lives.

There is something more about the nature of wisdom. Since the bible does not address specifically every situation we find ourselves in, we must go beyond hearing God's Word, to discerning His desire in these situations. For instance, should I move to this state? Should I take this job? Should I marry this person? Wisdom includes the mature judgment on what to do in these circumstances.

Let's make this year the year that we pursue wisdom and apply it to our lives!

Colossians 4:5; Hebrews 13:21; James 1:5

March 9

Daily Devotion for DESTINY:

Psalms 107:1 (The Amplified Bible, classic edition) -**1** O give thanks to the Lord, for He is good; for His mercy *and* loving-kindness endures forever!

Welcome to our Thankful Day! This is our day to not ask God for anything but thank Him for everything that He has done this week! If you are going through a rough time and are struggling to find a reason to thank God, just think about the fact that He is a good God.

God is so good that the scriptures (Lamentations 3:23) tells us that His mercy is new every morning. Both His mercy and loving kindness endures forever! God, I thank you for the mercy that you extend to me each day!

Let this be the year that we show God how thankful we are for His mercy by extending mercy to our brothers and sisters! This will certainly make God smile!

Psalms 118:1; I Chronicles 16:34; Luke 1:50

March 10

Daily Devotion for DESTINY:

I Timothy 6:12 (The Amplified Bible, classic edition) - **2** Fight the good fight of the faith; lay hold of the eternal life to which you were summoned and [for which] you confessed the good confession [of faith] before many witnesses.

Happy Faith Day! Are you in a spiritual battle this morning? The truth is that all of the battles we face are for one purpose and one purpose only. They come to steal our faith. satan knows that if he can make us believe that God is not really who He says He is and He is not really going to do what He says He will do, then he can defeat us.

Let's decide this year that we are not just going to fight to maintain our faith, but we are going to maintain our faith while we fight. When we keep our faith intact, we will win this battle!

Hebrews 3:14; Romans 10:9-10; II Timothy 4:7

March 11

Daily Devotion for DESTINY:

Ephesians 2:10 (New Living Translation) - **10** For we are God's masterpiece. He has created us anew in Christ Jesus, so we can do the good things he planned for us long ago.

Before we were born, God gave us specific spiritual gifts, abilities, passions and a unique personality. There is no one else exactly like you in this universe because there is no one else that has the exact same make-up as you do. The scriptures call us "God's masterpiece". This is why our destiny is so important. It is our destiny, and no one can fulfill it like we could.

Getting to our destiny is a journey (process). We make daily decisions towards this journey each and every day. If we do not go through the process, we will not have the power that it takes to be effective in our destiny. Remember, our destiny is not only for us. Someone, somewhere is waiting on you to reach your destination!

Be determined that this is the year that you are going to take the steps necessary to not only lead you to your destiny, but to make you effective once you have reached your destination!

Philippians 2:13; Colossians 1:10; Hebrews 13:21

March 12

Daily Devotion for DESTINY:

Hebrews 4:12 (The Amplified Bible, classic edition) - **12** For the Word that God speaks is alive and full of power [making it active, operative, energizing, and effective]; it is sharper than any two-edged sword, penetrating to the dividing line of the [a]breath of life (soul) and [the immortal] spirit, and of joints and marrow [of the deepest parts of our nature], exposing *and* sifting *and* analyzing *and* judging the very thoughts and purposes of the heart.

I would like to talk about a very important attribute that we must have to pursue our destiny: DISCERNMENT! When we received Jesus as our Lord and Savior, we are given special ability and the responsibility to see the heart of an issue.

We must be able to discern the Will of God, separate truth from error and identify the voice of the Holy Spirit as He leads us. As we transform and renew our minds with the Word of God, we will find that our discernment will increase.

Let's make this the year that we increase our intake of the Word of God which in turn will increase our discernment.

March 13

Daily Devotion for DESTINY:

Psalms 19:14 (The Amplified Bible, classic edition) - **14** Let the words of my mouth and the meditation of my heart be acceptable in Your sight, O Lord, my [firm, impenetrable] Rock and my Redeemer.

Happy Meditation Day! If you really want to grow in God's grace, invite Him into the deepest recesses of your heart. This is where God does His best work. We must obey God not only in word or deed, but in our thoughts.

We recognize that God knows everything about us anyway, but He does not go where He is not invited. Inviting God into the meditation of our heart (our thought life) proves that we are dependent upon Him.

Let this be the year that we meditate on the Word of God and in turn perfect our thought life into one that is acceptable to God. When we do this, our words and deeds will follow.

Psalms 104:34; Philippians 4:8; Psalms 49:3

March 14

Daily Devotion for DESTINY:

Romans 10:9-10 (The Amplified Bible) - **9** Because if you acknowledge *and* confess with your lips that Jesus is Lord and, in your heart, believe (adhere to, trust in, and rely on the truth) that God raised Him from the dead, you will be saved. **10** For with the heart a person believes (adheres to, trusts in, and relies on Christ) and so is justified (declared righteous, acceptable to God), and with the mouth he confesses (declares openly and speaks out freely his faith) *and* confirms [his] salvation.

Good morning! It is Transformation Day! The biblical definition of transformation is "Change or renewal from a life that no longer conforms to the ways of the world to a life that pleases God. Our scripture today tells us how to start our journey of transformation.

If you have not yet received Jesus as Lord and Savior of your life, there is no better time than the present to do so. All you have to do is confess that Jesus is Lord with your mouth and believe in your heart that God raised Him from the dead. This is the beginning of a transformed life.

Let's make this the year that we not only begin this transformation journey but continue to transform our life through the Word of God!

Romans 1:16-17; I peter 1:23; Acts 16:31

March 15

Daily Devotion for DESTINY:

Proverbs 19:20 (The Amplified Bible, classic edition) - **20** Hear counsel, receive instruction, *and* accept correction, that you may be wise in the time to come.

Happy Wisdom Day! We do not get wisdom on our own, nor does it come to us by accident. We must actively pursue wisdom. We pursue wisdom by meditating and applying the Word of God to our lives, but wisdom also comes from Godly counsel. God sends divine connections to us for this very reason.

Perhaps you are someone's divine connection. Let's make sure that we continue to grow in wisdom this year so that we can impart the wisdom that we gain to whomever God sends to us!

Proverbs 12:15; Proverbs 4:1; Psalms 90:12

March 16

Daily Devotion for DESTINY:

Ephesians 1:3 (The Living Bible) - **3** How we praise God, the Father of our Lord Jesus Christ, who has blessed us with every blessing in heaven because we belong to Christ.

Good morning! It is Thankful Day! Thankfulness should be a way of life for the children of God. Why? One reason is because God has blessed us with every blessing that is in heaven through His son, Jesus!

Jesus teaches us in Matthew 6:10 to pray these blessings down from heaven so that they will be manifested in the earth.

Let us think about all of the things that God has already given us, then think on all of the things that He desires to give to us. When we do that, thankfulness is the only appropriate response which will manifest itself in praise. Praise Ye the Lord!

Genesis 22:18; II Corinthians 1:3; John 10:29-30

March 17

Daily Devotion for DESTINY:

St. John 20:29 (The Living Bible) - **29** Then Jesus told him, "You believe because you have seen me. But blessed are those who haven't seen me and believe anyway."

Happy Faith Day! We have often heard the term "seeing is believing". As children of God, we believe the opposite is true. We do not have to see to believe.

Jesus did not criticize Thomas for wanting to see and touch. He understood that was a natural human desire; however, Jesus praised those that believe without seeing. This means that you have unshakeable faith! You have undeniable trust in God. We get this faith by hearing (with our hearts) the Word of God.

Let's make this the year that we meditate on and really hear (with our hearts) the Word of God. In doing so, we will develop unshakeable faith!

I Peter 1:8; II Corinthians 5:7; Hebrews 11:1

March 18

Daily Devotion for DESTINY:

Genesis 1:27-28 (The Message Bible) - **26-28** God spoke: "Let us make human beings in our image, make them reflecting our nature So they can be responsible for the fish in the sea, the birds in the air, the cattle, And, yes, Earth itself, and every animal that moves on the face of Earth." God created human beings; He created them Godlike, Reflecting God's nature. He created them male and female. God bless them: "Prosper! Reproduce! Fill Earth! Take charge! Be responsible for fish in the sea and birds in the air, for every living thing that moves on the face of Earth."

This morning, I would like to speak to the spirit of creativity that is within you. God is a creative God and He has passed his creativity to His children. We were designed to reflect God's nature. This upsets satan, so he desires to destroy the creativity that is within us. Our creativity is what makes us unique.

We oftentimes do not see the creative ability that is within us. As we seek the Lord about our destiny; He will reveal His purpose for the creativity that He has placed in each and every one of us. What has God called you to create? The creative tasks that God has assigned to you will build the Kingdom.

This year, let's stir up our creative ability to reflect the purpose that God has called us to. The World needs you!

Ephesians 2:10; Isaiah 43:7; Psalms 139:14

March 19

Daily Devotion for DESTINY:

John 16:13 (English Standard Version) - **13** When the Spirit of truth comes, he will guide you into all the truth, for he will not speak on his own authority, but whatever he hears he will speak, and he will declare to you the things that are to come.

In order to succeed in life, we must not be afraid to ask for help. Our scripture today is Jesus talking to His disciples the night before He is crucified. They are scared, discouraged, shocked and confused about Jesus' upcoming crucifixion.

Jesus consoled them by letting them know that He will not leave them alone, Just as He has not left us alone. He has sent us a comforter that is not only with us, but He is within us. Are you scared, lonely, discouraged, confused? Call upon Him and He will answer you!

John 14:26; John 14:17; John 12:49

March 20

Daily Devotion for DESTINY:

John 15:7 (The Amplified Bible, classic edition) - **7** If you live in Me [abide vitally united to Me] and My words remain in you *and* continue to live in your hearts, ask whatever you will, and it shall be done for you.

Happy Meditation Day! There is a difference between getting and the Word of God and the Word of God getting in you. Our scripture this morning admonishes us to meditate on the Word of God and allow it to get into us.

You will find that as you meditate on God's word, your will and desires change from what you once desired to what God desires for you. Now that your desires are according to God's purpose for your life, you can ask anything,` and God will do it for you!

Let's make this the year that we fine tune our desires by meditating on God's word and watch Him manifest Himself in our lives!

I John 5:14; Galatians 5:36; Matthew 7:7

March 21

Daily Devotion for DESTINY:

Acts 1:8 (The Amplified Bible, classic edition) - **8** But you shall receive power (ability, efficiency, and might) when the Holy Spirit has come upon you, and you shall be My witnesses in Jerusalem and all Judea and Samaria and to the ends (the very bounds) of the earth.

Good morning! It is Transformation Day! We have been working on transforming our minds through the Word of God. Another very important element of our transformation is the Holy Spirit.

The Holy Spirit is the third person of the Godhead that the Father and Son promised to send to live in everyone who has accepted Jesus as their Lord and Savior. He serves many functions in our lives, but one of His main functions is to empower us to live a holy life, which in turn makes us effective witnesses.

Let us make this year the year that we accept the gift of the Holy Spirit and we become even more effective as we witness to family, friends and everyone that God sends across our paths!

Mark 16:15; Matthew 28:19; John 15:27

March 22

Daily Devotion for DESTINY:

Proverbs 17:28 (The Amplified Bible, classic edition) - **28** Even a fool when he holds his peace is considered wise; when he closes his lips, he is esteemed a man of understanding.

Happy Wisdom Day! It is wise to observe but say very little. We learn by listening not talking. There is a reason that we have two ears and only one mouth.

We should think before we speak. If what we are about to say is not edifying or profitable, then we should not say that. The tongue is a dangerous little member that can easily hurt others. Wise men and women hold their tongues.

This year, lets grow in wisdom by hearing more and talking less. In doing so, we honor God!

Job 13:5; Ecclesiastes 10:14; Proverbs 15:2

March 23

Daily Devotion for DESTINY:

I Thessalonians 5:18 (The Amplified Bible, classic edition) - **18** Thank [God] in everything [no matter what the circumstances may be, be thankful and give thanks], for this is the will of God for you [who are] in Christ Jesus [the Revealer and Mediator of that will].

Good morning! It is Thankful Day! Notice that our scripture today says "in" everything give thanks and not "for" everything give thanks. One Pastor says that this is because everything is not God sent, but everything is God used. I wholeheartedly agree!

What this means is that God does not necessarily send all of the trials and tribulations that we encounter: however, He does take the opportunities to teach us a lesson or even just show us that He has our back while we go through them.

This year, lets thank God even in our trials and tribulations. This is His will concerning us!

Colossians 3:17; Ephesians 5:20; Philippians 4:6

March 24

Daily Devotion for DESTINY:

Matthew 14:28-31 (English Standard Version) - [28]And Peter answered him, "Lord, if it is you, command me to come to you on the water." [29] He said, "Come." So Peter got out of the boat and walked on the water and came to Jesus. [30] But when he saw the wind,[a] he was afraid, and beginning to sink he cried out, "Lord, save me." [31]Jesus immediately reached out his hand and took hold of him, saying to him, "O you of little faith, why did you doubt?"

Happy Faith Day! The storm that the disciples encountered in this scripture was not the first storm that they had been through, Disciples are expected to imitate their teacher, so when Peter saw Jesus walking on water, He wanted to walk on water too!

Many people focus on the fact that Peter began to sink, but I applaud Peter for being willing to get out of the boat! Jesus gently reprimanded Peter for letting his faith slip after all of the miracles that he had the opportunity to witness.

Let us make this the year that we imitate our teacher by stepping out of our natural faith and into Supernatural faith and watch God work!

James 1:6-8; Matthew 8:26; Matthew 6:30

March 25

Daily Devotion for DESTINY:

Matthew 9:16-17 (English Standard Version) – [16] No one puts a piece of unshrunk cloth on an old garment, for the patch tears away from the garment, and a worse tear is made. [17] Neither is new wine put into old wineskins. If it is, the skins burst and the wine is spilled and the skins are destroyed. But new wine is put into fresh wineskins, and so both are preserved."

In this parable that Jesus taught, the new wine represents the inner aspects of a Christian life and the new cloth represents our outward actions and conversations. Our behavior reflects our commitment to God.

Our past sinful life (the old cloth and the old wine) cannot be repaired. It must be replaced with a new life in Christ (the new wine and the new cloth). Jesus is trying to teach us that our life cannot be a mixture of two opposite principles. We must choose ye this day who we are going to serve (Joshua 24:15).

Let's make this year the year that we replace old wineskins with new wineskins so that we can walk totally in the newness of life!

I Corinthians 3:1-2; John 16:12; Isaiah 40:11

March 26

Daily Devotion for DESTINY:

James 4:10 (The Amplified Bible, classic edition) - **10** Humble yourselves [feeling very insignificant] in the presence of the Lord, and He will exalt you [He will lift you up and make your lives significant].

To humble yourself before the Lord means that we recognize the greatness of God and we recognize that we need Him. We acknowledge that we are sinful and unworthy. We submit to God and understand that we can do nothing without Him. We are dependent upon God and realize that we are constantly in need of His grace and mercy.

The scripture says that when we come to the Lord in this way, He will lift us up out of our circumstances and cause the greatness that He has put in us to manifest!

This year, let's humble ourselves before that Lord and allow Him to pull out everything that He put in us to live a healthy, prosperous life on this earth. This is how we glorify God!

I Peter 5:6; Matthew 23:12; Luke 14:11

March 27

Daily Devotion for DESTINY:

Isaiah 26:3 (The Amplified Bible, classic edition) - **3** You will guard him *and* keep him in perfect *and* constant peace whose mind [both its inclination and its character] is stayed on You, because he commits himself to You, leans on You, *and* hopes confidently in You.

Good morning on this Meditation Day! Are you in need of peace this morning? God promises that He will keep us in perfect peace if we keep our minds focused on Him.

We keep our focus on God by meditating on His word. Our minds are one of the greatest tools that God has given us. Anything that we feed will grow and anything that we starve will die.

Let's make this year the year that we feed our minds by meditating on God's word. In doing so, our faith will increase and our doubts will starve to death. Nothing will be impossible to us because we walk in peace knowing that God is ordering each and every step!

Philippians 4:7; John 16:33; Romans 5:1

March 28

Daily Devotion for DESTINY:

Philippians 2:5 (The Amplified Bible, classic edition) -
5 Let this attitude *and* purpose *and* [humble] mind be in you which was in Christ Jesus: [Let Him be your example in humility:]

It is Transformation Day! Our scripture today is telling us that we must transform our minds into the mind of Christ. What was the mind of Christ? The scripture goes on to say that Jesus humbled himself by laying down His status as the son of God and was obedient to God all the way to the cross!

We meditate on the word day and night to transform our minds into the mind of Christ and become obedient to Him all the way to our God ordained destination.

This year, let's develop the mind of Christ so that we possess God's character in our actions and our attitudes.

I John 2:6; I Peter 2:21; Ephesians 5:2

March 29

Daily Devotion for DESTINY:

Proverbs 10:14 (The Amplified Bible, classic edition) - **14** Wise men store up knowledge [in mind and heart], but the mouth of the foolish is a present destruction.

Welcome to a wonderful Wisdom Day! Wise men (and women) store up knowledge that they receive by meditating on the Word of God, prayer and talking to other wise men. They value this knowledge so much that they store it in their hearts and minds.

Foolish men (and women) speak everything that comes to their minds. They have no filter. This causes destruction in their lives spiritually, mentally and sometimes physically.

Let's make this year the year that we become wiser by not only meditating on the Word of God, but also by seeking out wise men and women to pour into our lives. These are our divine connections.

Matthew 12:35; Proverbs 21:23; Proverbs 1:5

March 30

Daily Devotion for DESTINY:

I Thessalonians 5:16-17 (The Amplified Bible, classic edition) - **16** Be happy [in your faith] *and* rejoice *and* be glad-hearted continually (always); **17** Be unceasing in prayer [praying perseveringly]

It is Thankful Day! We are on a journey this year to fulfill the will of God for our lives. We do not all have the same destiny and we are not all in the same place on our journey.

Our scripture today is God's will for each and every one of us! We are to rejoice ALWAYS! We are to pray WITHOUT CEASING! And we are to give thank in All of our circumstances!

Let's do our best to fulfill the will of God in these areas of our lives this year.

Philippians 4:8; Matthew 5:12; Luke 10:20

March 31

Daily Devotion for DESTINY:

Ephesians 6:16(New King James Version) - **16** above all, taking the shield of faith with which you will be able to quench all the fiery darts of the wicked one.

Happy Faith Day! Are we fully dressed this morning? Do we have on our shield of faith? We have a real enemy whose goal is to destroy us. We must make sure that we put on our shield of faith every morning to quench the fiery darts of the enemy.

That is why it is so important to spend time with God each and every day. Make sure that the time you spend with God includes meditating on His word because faith comes by hearing and hearing by the Word of God.

Let us make this year the year that we put on our full armor each day! Don't leave home without it!

Genesis 15:1; Proverbs 18:10; I Peter 5:8-9

April

so is my word that goes out from my mouth:
It will not return to me empty,
but will accomplish what I desire
and achieve the purpose for which I sent it.

Isaiah 55:11 (NIV)

April 1

Daily Devotion for DESTINY:

Genesis 22:9-12 (English Standard Version) - ⁹When they came to the place of which God had told him, Abraham built the altar there and laid the wood in order and bound Isaac his son and laid him on the altar, on top of the wood. ¹⁰ Then Abraham reached out his hand and took the knife to slaughter his son. ¹¹ But the angel of the Lᴏʀᴅ called to him from heaven and said, "Abraham, Abraham!" And he said, "Here I am." ¹² He said, "Do not lay your hand on the boy or do anything to him, for now I know that you fear God, seeing you have not withheld your son, your only son, from me."

Our scripture today focuses not only on hearing the voice of God, but CONTINUALLY hearing the voice of God. God was not only testing Abraham's faith, but He was also testing Abraham's ability to hear him. Abraham heard and obeyed God when He told him to sacrifice his son, but what if he had not heard God when He told him to stay his hand? Abraham would have killed his future!

It is important that we hear and obey every word that precedes out of the mouth of God so that we do not kill our future. Let's make this the year that we perfect hearing AND obeying God's voice so that He can bring us to our expected end!

Genesis 26:5; Hebrews 11:19; James 2:18

April 2

Daily Devotion for DESTINY:

John 14:27 (English Standard Version) – ^{27} Peace I leave with you; my peace I give to you. Not as the world gives do I give to you. Let not your hearts be troubled, neither let them be afraid.

Jesus was about to die and leave His disciples. In His last Will and Testament, He left something that was very important to Him.... PEACE. Peace is also our inheritance.

The peace of God is not like the peace that the world gives us. The peace of the world is dependent on circumstances, but the peace of God is with us in spite of circumstances.

Our Father has left us rich! Let's claim our inheritance this year and walk in the peace that surpasses all understanding!

Philippians 4:7; John 17:33; Colossians 3:15

April 3

Daily Devotion for DESTINY:

Romans 8:5-6 (New King James Version) -**5** For those who live according to the flesh set their minds on the things of the flesh, but those *who live* according to the Spirit, the things of the Spirit. **6** For to be carnally minded *is* death, but to be spiritually minded *is* life and peace.

Happy Meditation Day! God often presents us with options on how to live our lives. He gives us free wills because He wants us to choose to live for Him.

So it is with our scripture today. We can choose to set our minds (meditate) on the things of the flesh (and be carnally minded), or we can choose to set our minds (meditate) on the things of the Spirit (and be Spiritually minded).

This year, let us choose to be Spiritually minded so that we can live a life of peace and please our God in the process!

Galatians 5:19-25; I Corinthians 2:14; John 3:6

April 4

Daily Devotion for DESTINY:

Psalms 51:10 (The Amplified Bible, classic edition) -**10** Create in me a clean heart, O God, and renew a right, persevering, *and* steadfast spirit within me.

It is Transformation Day! Our scripture today was written by David after he committed what we would consider a huge sin! David was a man after God's own heart. Not because he did not sin, but because he was quick to repent. When we repent, God is faithful and just to forgive us of our sins.

Has your heart been broken? Are you carrying things in your heart that is making you sick? Only God can create a new heart within you. Just ask Him.

Let us make this year the year that we allow God to create a new heart within us. This is the ultimate transformation!

Ezekiel 11:19; Matthew 5:18; Acts 15:9

April 5

Daily Devotion for DESTINY:

Luke 2:52 (The Amplified Bible, classic edition) - **52** And Jesus increased in wisdom (in broad and full understanding) and in stature *and* years, and in favor with God and man.

Happy Wisdom Day! Many people interpret this verse as saying that Jesus increased in knowledge; however, the scripture says that Jesus grew in wisdom and stature. Wisdom and knowledge are two different things. Wisdom is the ability to apply knowledge.

It is very important to gain knowledge by meditating on the Word of God and gleaning from the experiences and instructions of our divine connections, but it is even more important to learn how to apply the knowledge that we gain.

This year, let's focus on growing in wisdom. This will cause us to have favor with both God and man!

I Samuel 2:26; Luke 1:80; Luke 2:40

April 6

Daily Devotion for DESTINY:

Colossians 3:15 (The Amplified Bible, classic edition) - **15** And let the peace (soul harmony which comes) from Christ rule (act as umpire continually) in your hearts [deciding and settling with finality all questions that arise in your minds, in that peaceful state] to which as [members of Christ's] one body you were also called [to live]. And be thankful (appreciative), [giving praise to God always].

Good morning and welcome to Thankful Day! Last week, we learned that Jesus left us peace in His last Will and Testament. Have you claimed your inheritance yet?

Nothing promotes peace more than gratitude to God for His mercy. We are only able to be thankful to the extent that we trust God.

This year we are going to develop a spirit of thankfulness and let God reward us with His peace!

Philippians 4:7; I Thessalonians 5:18; Romans 15:13

April 7

Daily Devotion for DESTINY:

I Peter 1:8-9 (New International Version) - **8** Though you have not seen him, you love him; and even though you do not see him now, you believe in him and are filled with an inexpressible and glorious joy, **9** for you are receiving the end result of your faith, the salvation of your souls.

Happy Faith Day! Faith causes us to act on what we hear in our spirit; believe the promises of God that has not yet been fulfilled and trust God in the midst of trying circumstances.

Though we have not seen God, we believe Him. This causes us to have unexplainable joy. This joy is the end result of our faith in God.

This year, let us take a leap of faith and allow God to turn the dreams and visions that He has given us into reality.

John 20:29; II Corinthians 5:7; II Corinthians 4:18

April 8

Daily Devotion for DESTINY:

Revelation 3:8 (The Amplified Bible, classic edition) - **8** I know your [record of] works *and* what you are doing. See! I have set before you a door wide open which no one is able to shut; I know that you have but little power, and yet you have kept My Word *and* guarded My message and have not renounced *or* denied My name.

I heard this scripture in my spirit when I woke up this morning and wanted to share. God is opening doors for us that no man can shut. Do not let fear discourage you from walking through the doors that God is opening. Many times we wait on God to place us in the open doors, but most of the time, He puts the door within our reach and we must walk through it.

God also closes doors for us. Please know that when God closes a door, it is not rejection; it is just direction! It is very important to know the difference between the doors that God is opening and the doors that God is closing. We learn the difference by communing with Him day after day.

Let us make this year the year that we begin to walk through the doors that God is opening and allow the world to see that you are loved by your Father! NO FEAR LIVES HERE!!!!

I Corinthians 16:9; John 17:6; Philippians 4:13

April 9

Daily Devotion for DESTINY:

3 John 1:2 (King James Version) -**2** Beloved, I wish above all things that thou mayest prosper and be in health, even as thy soul prospers.

Our Scripture today lets us know God's will for us concerning money. We often misinterpret I Timothy 6:10 to say that money is the root of all evil when the scripture says that the LOVE of money is the root of all evil.

It is God's desire that we prosper financially and be in health AS our soul (mind, will and emotions) prosper. God is all about the total man (and woman) being healthy. It takes finances to walk in God's plan for our lives. How can we help our brothers and sisters when we are struggling ourselves?

This year, lets allow God to prosper our total man so that we can fulfill our total destiny.

II Peter 3:18; 2 Thessalonians 2:13; Philippians 2:4

April 10

Daily Devotion for DESTINY:

Colossians 3:2 (The Amplified Bible, classic edition) - **2** And set your minds *and* keep them set on what is above (the higher things), not on the things that are on the earth.

Happy Meditation Day! Our minds are very powerful; therefore, the thoughts that we allow to stay in our minds are very important. You can't stop a thought from entering your mind, but you can choose to keep it moving!

This is the season to remove all distractions out of our lives so that we can organize our thoughts and meditate on the things that God is speaking to us. You are only one thought away from a total transformation in your life.

This year, let's become intentional about the things that we think and meditate on.

I Chronicles 22:19; Matthew 16:22; Philippians 3:19

April 11

Daily Devotion for DESTINY:

II Corinthians 3:18 (English Standard Version) - [18]Let no one deceive himself. If anyone among you thinks that he is wise in this age, let him become a fool that he may become wise.

Good morning! It is Transformation Day! God is continually working in the lives of His children to bring about a transformation. He wants us to reflect His likeness and His image. Our goal is to be like mirrors. We want to reflect the glory of the Lord.

Our scripture today shows our progression as we transform into God's image. First, we behold the glory; second, we reflect the glory and finally we become the glory when we go home to be with Jesus!

Are you willing to allow God to transform you into His image? This year, let's submit to the transformation process so that we reflect Christ.

I Corinthians 13:12; Romans 8:29; Romans 13:14

April 12

Daily Devotion for DESTINY:

Proverbs 11:30 (The Amplified Bible, classic edition) - **30** The fruit of the [uncompromisingly] righteous is a tree of life, and he who is wise captures human lives [for God, as a fisher of men—he gathers and receives them for eternity].

It is Wisdom Day! Many people interpret our scripture today to say that if a man wins souls, he is wise. That is not what the scripture actually says and that is not necessarily true. What the scripture says is that if you are wise, you will win souls.

A wise man (or woman) does not even have to speak directly to you to win your soul. We are attracted to wisdom. It tends to capture our attention and earn our confidence. An example of this would be the Pastors and teachers that we watch on television and on social media. They are not speaking directly to us (in many cases), but they are speaking to our souls.

Let's make this year the year that we grow in wisdom and win souls for the Lord. Our goal this year is that "Each One, Reach One"!

Proverbs 3:18; Daniel 12:3; Proverbs 15:4

April 13

Daily Devotion for DESTINY:

Psalms 100:3-5 (The Amplified Bible, classic edition) -**3** Know (perceive, recognize, and understand with approval) that the Lord is God! It is He Who has made us, not we ourselves [and we are His]! We are His people and the sheep of His pasture.

4 Enter into His gates with thanksgiving *and* a thank offering and into His courts with praise! Be thankful *and* say so to Him, bless *and* affectionately praise His name!

5 For the Lord is good; His mercy *and* loving-kindness are everlasting; His faithfulness *and* truth endure to all generations.

Welcome to Thankful Day! Our praise and the motivation behind it is very important to God. We are called upon to praise God. Just in case you need it, verse 5 supplies us with just a few of the many reasons we should praise Him.

We all have individual assignments in life, but we also all have one assignment in common. Isaiah 43:7 tells us that we were created for God's glory; therefore, the assignment that we all have in common is to glorify God.

Let's make this year the year that we glorify our God by elevating our praise to Him!

Psalms 98:4; Psalms 146:1; Psalms 66:4

April 14

Daily Devotion for DESTINY:

Mark 11:24 (The Amplified Bible, classic edition) - **24** For this reason I am telling you, whatever you ask for in prayer, believe (trust and be confident) that it is granted to you, and you will [get it].

Happy Faith Day! What does prayer have to do with our faith? Everything! God loves it when we show our faith in Him by coming to Him in prayer.

You will find that as you build your faith in God by reading, hearing and meditating on His word; your prayer life will increase in quantity and quality. In other words, we will pray more often and more accurately because we are praying God's will and believing it will come to pass!

Let's make this year the year that we step up our prayer life because we believe God!

Matthew 21:22; I John 5:14; John 14:13

April 15

Daily Devotion for DESTINY:

Matthew 26:38-39 (The Amplified Bible, classic edition) - **38** Then He said to them, My soul is very sad *and* deeply grieved, so that [a]I am almost dying of sorrow. Stay here and keep awake *and* keep watch with Me.**39** And going a little farther, He threw Himself upon the ground on His face and prayed saying, My Father, if it is possible, let this cup pass away from Me; nevertheless, not what I will [not what I desire], but as You will *and* desire.

The fact that Jesus was a human and experienced the same struggles as we do is evident in today's scripture. Although His Spirit was willing, Jesus' flesh did not want to do the very thing that He was created to do (die for our sins), but He wrestled His flesh in prayer until His Spirit won. Then, He was able to say, "Not my will, but thy will be done'!

On our journey to our destiny, we are going to experience all of the emotions that Jesus experienced and more. When we do, we must do just as Jesus did and labor in prayer until our spirits become submissive to the will of our Father.

Let's make this year the year that we win the battle over our flesh until we are able to say, "Not my will God, but your will be done in my life"!

John 12:27; I Peter 4:7; Matthew 25:13

April 16

Daily Devotion for DESTINY:

Luke 24:5-6 (New King James Version) - Then, as they were afraid and bowed *their* faces to the earth, they said to them, "Why do you seek the living among the dead? **6** He is not here but is risen! Remember how He spoke to you when He was still in Galilee.

It was completely logical for the women to go to Jesus' tomb early that first Resurrection morning. After all, they had witnessed their Lord and Savior die and be buried there just a few days earlier. They went to do the final thing that they could do for Him.

Even though Jesus told them that He would be resurrected, they were still surprised on several fronts once they arrived at the tomb. First, they tomb was open and Jesus was not in it. Second, They were greeted by angels who asked them a question that still penetrates our hearts to this day…"Why do you seek the living amongst the dead"?

Are you seeking for Jesus where He cannot be found (amongst the dead)? To some, Jesus is just a historic figure only to be found in archives. To me, He is a living God who lives in me!

Mark 16:5-6; Matthew 28:3-5; Revelation 2:8

April 17

Daily Devotion for DESTINY:

II Timothy 2:15 (King James Version) - **15** Study to shew thyself approved unto God, a workman that needeth not to be ashamed, rightly dividing the word of truth.

It is Meditation Day! The word study in this scripture means to be diligent; continue the practice of; or to meditate. When we meditate on the word of God, we will find that we engage with God in a deeper way.

We will begin to experience more of His love. We will build our faith, but most of all, we will come to know Him more intimately. Meditation cannot be done in a hurry. It takes some time. If we want to be successful in both our natural and our spiritual lives, we must carve out some time for God each and every day.

Let's make this year is the year that we show ourselves approved unto God by meditating on His word.

II Peter 1:10; II Corinthians 10:18; II Peter 3:14

April 18

Daily Devotion for DESTINY:

Ezekiel 36:26 (King James Version) - **26** A new heart also will I give you, and a new spirit will I put within you: and I will take away the stony heart out of your flesh, and I will give you an heart of flesh.

It is Transformation Day! Since each of us is unique, God's process to for Himself in us is unique as well. Even though the Spirit of God is the one that transforms our souls, we must take personal responsibility of the process.

It can take a lifetime for the Spirit of God to totally transform our lives to line up with the word of God. We cooperate with the Spirit when we become not only hearers, but doers of the word (James 1:22).

This year, lets allow the Holy spirit to transform our hearts that have been broken into hearts that are sensitive to the things of God.

Ezekiel 11:19-20; Psalms 51:10; II Corinthians 5:17

April 19

Daily Devotion for DESTINY:

Ecclesiastes 2:26 (The Amplified Bible, classic edition) - **26** For to the person who pleases Him God gives wisdom and knowledge and joy; but to the sinner He gives the work of gathering and heaping up, that he may give to one who pleases God. This also is vanity and a striving after the wind *and* a feeding on it.

Happy Wisdom Day! Our scripture today was written by the wisest man of his time, Solomon. Solomon learned that seeking pleasure as a way of life did not satisfy him. Even though he had wealth and fame, he did not have joy, peace or happiness.

Solomon found out that without the wisdom and knowledge of God, there is not enjoyment of the good things in life. After all, it is God that gives us the wisdom and knowledge that leads to our joy in life.

This year, let's seek first the Kingdom (and wisdom) of God so that everything else will be added unto us (Matthew 6:33).

Job 27:16-17; John 16:24; James 3:17

April 20

Daily Devotion for DESTINY:

Psalms 118:24 (King James Version) - **24** This is the day which the Lord hath made; we will rejoice and be glad in it.

It is Thankful Day! What day is the day that the Lord has made? Today and every day! I am a planner. I like to plan every aspect of my day. I cannot count the times that God has changed my plans.

I have learned and am still learning that whatever the day has in store for me, I am to rejoice and be glad in it. Why? Because I know that God ordained this day and with Him, I will have victory today and every day.

Let us raise our praise this year as we allow God to order our steps each and every day!

Nehemiah 8:10; Revelation 1:10; Psalms 84:10

April 21

Daily Devotion for DESTINY:

John 6:35 (The Amplified Bible, classic edition) - **35** Jesus replied, I am the Bread of Life. He who comes to Me will never be hungry, and he who believes in *and* cleaves to *and* trusts in *and* relies on Me will never thirst any more (at any time).

You made it to Faith Day! In the natural, bread and water satisfies our flesh. The same is true in the Spirit. Jesus lets us know that He is our bread and water. If we have faith in Him, we will never be hungry or thirsty again.

The crowd that Jesus was talking to in our scripture today only had interest in their physical needs. They lacked the perception that Jesus was more interested in their spiritual needs and so it is today.

Let us make this year the year that we trust God with both our natural and our spiritual needs. The sooner that we understand that our life is totally dependent upon God, the happier we will be!

John 6:41; Revelation 22:17; John 7:37-38

April 22

Daily Devotion for DESTINY:

Joshua 1:5 (The Amplified Bible, classic edition) - **5** No man shall be able to stand before you all the days of your life. As I was with Moses, so I will be with you; I will not fail you or forsake you.

In our scripture today, Joshua had taken Moses' place as the leader of the Children of Israel. Joshua was not Moses and guess what? The Lord anointed and appointed him anyway! It is wonderful to admire your mentors and predecessors. While doing so, keep in mind your own individuality and uniqueness.

God chose you for this time and season because He needs the anointing that He deposited in you for this hour. As long as we are operating in the power that God has given us, no force will be able to stand against us. He will always be with us.

This year, let us choose to be an original and not a carbon copy. God needs you!

Matthew 28:20; Deuteronomy 31:6-8; Joshua 1:9

April 23

Daily Devotion for DESTINY:

Luke 9:62 (The Amplified Bible, classic edition) - **62** Jesus said to him, No one who puts his hand to the plow and looks back [to the things behind] is fit for the kingdom of God.

Jesus' message in this scripture is to keep your focus. It is so easy to get distracted by the cares of this life. As Christians, we cannot go towards the Kingdom with our hearts and minds fixed on what we left behind.

In our walk with Christ, we must keep our eyes focused on Him. Do not continue looking back longing for the things that could not go with us in our new season.

Let's make this year the year that we focus on the path that God has for us and never look back!

Philippians 3:13; Hebrews 10:38; Luke 17:31-32

April 24

Daily Devotion for DESTINY:

Psalms 119:15 (King James Version) - **15** I will meditate in thy precepts and have respect unto thy ways.

It is Meditation Day! The importance of meditating and fixing our eyes upon the Lord has really been on my heart. God does not ask us to do something that is not within our power to do. We can do all things through Christ who strengthens us.

The thing that we meditate on will become the dominating force in our lives. If we meditate on our past, it won't be long before we are re-living our past. By the same token, if we meditate on our future, it won't be long before we will be living in our destiny.

This year, let's forget those things that are behind and focus on those things that are in front of us!

Psalms 1:2; Psalms 119:97; James 1:25

April 25

Daily Devotion for DESTINY:

Acts 3:19 (The Amplified Bible, classic edition) - **19** So repent (change your mind and purpose); turn around *and* return [to God], that your sins may be erased (blotted out, wiped clean), that times of refreshing (of recovering from the effects of heat, of [a]reviving with fresh air) may come from the presence of the Lord.

It is Transformation Day! Our transformation begins when we repent and turn our lives over to God. Since the beginning of time, God's purpose has been to bring mankind back into harmony with Him.

Even though God's purpose began before time, He has revealed His purpose to His children. Each one of us has a part to play in bringing not lonely mankind, but the earth back into harmony with God. It is called our destiny.

This year, let's allow God to transform us, then reveal to us our assignment!

Isaiah 44:22; Psalms 51:9; Matthew 18:13

April 26

Daily Devotion for DESTINY:

Proverbs 17:27-28 (English Standard Version) – **27** Whoever restrains his words has knowledge, and he who has a cool spirit is a man of understanding. **28** Even a fool who keeps silent is considered wise; when he closes his lips, he is deemed intelligent.

Happy Wisdom Day! We have all met people that will proudly tell you "If it comes to my mind, it comes out of my mouth!" Our scripture today tells us that even a fool is considered both wise and intelligent when he keeps quiet.

When we restrain our words, we have knowledge. It is a natural thing to like to hear your own voice. Wouldn't you rather use your words sparingly so that when you do speak, people will listen?

Declare and Decree that this year we will choose our words very carefully and when we do speak, our words will be filled with wisdom, knowledge and understanding!

James 1:19; Proverbs 14:29; Ecclesiastes 9:17

April 27

Daily Devotion for DESTINY:

Philippians 4:13 (The Amplified Bible, classic edition) - **13** I have strength for all things in Christ Who empowers me [I am ready for anything and equal to anything through Him Who [a]infuses inner strength into me; I am [b]self-sufficient in Christ's sufficiency].

It is Thankful Day! We have so much to be thankful for! Today, I want to focus on the fact that we serve a God that strengthens us to do everything that He has anointed and appointed us to do! He does not give us an assignment, then make us figure out how to get it done!

I we trust God to direct our paths and provide for us while we are on our journey, then we will surely reach our destination.

Let's make it a point every day this year to wake up thanking God for giving us the strength to fulfill His will for us each and every day!

Isaiah 41:10; Colossians 1:11; Ephesians 6:10

April 28

Daily Devotion for DESTINY:

Matthew 9:10 (English Standard Version) - **2** And behold, some people brought to him a paralytic, lying on a bed. And when Jesus saw their faith, he said to the paralytic, "Take heart, my son; your sins are forgiven."

Happy Faith Day! Does anybody else wonder why when the men brought the paralyzed man to Jesus, He acknowledged their faith the said, "Take heart, your sins are forgiven" instead of saying "Rise up and walk?"

Well, Jesus' disciples wondered the same thing. He explained to them that an important part of His destiny was to forgive sins. After this teachable moment, Jesus told the man to pick up his bed and go home; and the man did just that!

Forgiveness and healing is a package deal if you have the faith to believe it. This year, let's increase our faith to believe this and become healthy Christians!

Matthew 9:22; James 2:18; Matthew 8:10

April 29

Daily Devotion for DESTINY:

John 15:16 (The Amplified Bible, classic edition) - **16** You have not chosen Me, but I have chosen you and I have appointed you [I have planted you], that you might go and bear fruit *and* keep on bearing, and that your fruit may be lasting [that it may remain, abide], so that whatever you ask the Father in My Name [as [a]presenting all that I Am], He may give it to you.

This is another scripture that is often misinterpreted. Some seem to think that Jesus has already chosen those who will be saved. This could not be farther from the truth. The word "chosen" in the Greek is the same word as "elected". They are often used interchangeably throughout the scriptures.

What Jesus was saying is that Hi Apostles had not chosen Him to be their teacher and their guide, but He had chosen them to be His Apostles. Aren't you glad that God chose you?

We all have individual assignments, but there is one assignment that we all have in common. God has chosen (elected) us to bear fruit and our fruit will remain because we will pray them through! Are you up for the challenge?

John 13:18; Ephesians 2:10; Jeremiah 1:5-7

April 30

Daily Devotion for DESTINY:

I Peter 5:2-3 (The Amplified Bible, classic edition) - **2** Tend (nurture, guard, guide, and fold) the flock of God that is [your responsibility], not by coercion *or* constraint, but willingly; not dishonorably motivated by the advantages *and* profits [belonging to the office], but eagerly *and* cheerfully; **3** Not domineering [as arrogant, dictatorial, and overbearing persons] over those in your charge, but being examples (patterns and models of Christian living) to the flock (the congregation).

I want to take this time to give a shout out to my Pastor, Walter E. Jordan II. Jeremiah 3:15 tells us that God will give us Pastors after our own heart that will lead us by example. Pastor Walt is that Pastor for me.

Our scripture today tells us what this type of Pastor looks like. He / She does not command anything from you. After all, if God gives us free will, who am I to try to control your will? A good Pastor understands that you are pregnant with purpose from God (keeping in mind that God's assignment for us will build His Kingdom, not our own kingdom) and they are the midwife to help you birth your purpose and walk into your destiny.

This year, please be sure that you are in an atmosphere that encourages you to walk in your God-given destiny. Time is winding up!

Titus 1:7; Ezekiel 34:31; Jeremiah 3:15

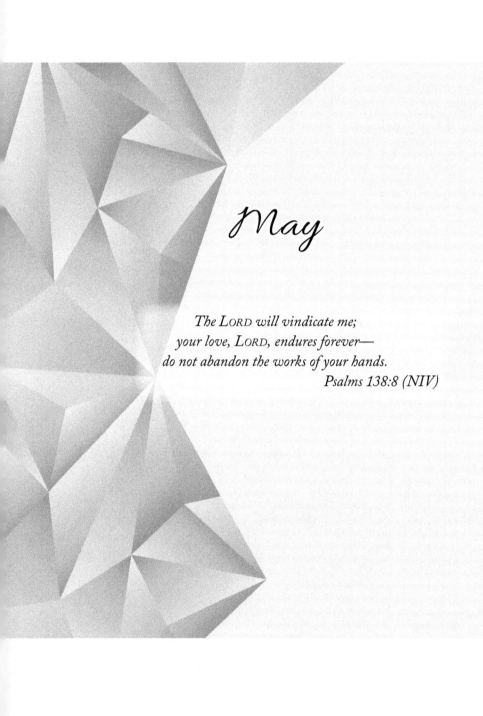

May

The LORD will vindicate me;
your love, LORD, endures forever—
do not abandon the works of your hands.

Psalms 138:8 (NIV)

May 1

Daily Devotion for DESTINY:

Psalms 145:5 (The Amplified Bible, classic edition) - **5** On the glorious splendor of Your majesty and on Your wondrous works I will meditate.

Good morning! It is Meditation Day! Let's start our week in praise! Our scripture today gives us just a couple of things that we can meditate on that will result in praise.

One songwriter said that when I think of the goodness of Jesus and all that He has done for me, my soul cries out hallelujah! I thank God for saving me! Can you imagine what would happen if we not only think on the goodness of Jesus, but meditate on it?

My challenge for you today is to spend the week meditating on just the goodness of God and watch what happens by the end of the week! Are you up for this challenge?

Isaiah 12:4; Daniel 4:37; Psalms 119:27

May 2

Daily Devotion for DESTINY:

Psalms 23:1-3 (English Standard Version) - The Lord is my shepherd; I shall not want. **2** He makes me lie down in green pastures. He leads me beside still waters .**3** He restores my soul. He leads me in paths of righteousness for his name's sake.

It is Transformation Day! We are meditating on a very familiar scripture today. So many of us are going through so much and need our souls (mind, will, and emotions) to be restored (transformed).

This Psalm was written by David as he reflected on how God transformed him through all of his trials and tribulations. He now understands that for every trial that he came through, a transformation took place in his soul.

As we go through our trials and tribulations this year, let's rest in God and allow Him to restore (transform) our minds, will and emotions.

John 10:11; Isaiah 40:11; John 10:14

May 3

Daily Devotion for DESTINY:

Proverbs 12:15 (English Standard Version) - **15** The way of a fool is right in his own eyes, but a wise man listens to advice.

Happy Wisdom Day! What keeps a wise man from being a fool? He not only listens to Godly advice, but he actually applies it to his life.

A fool, according to the bible, is one who does not ask for wisdom from above. He does not seek Godly Counsel. He walks in his own way so long that he thinks it is the right way.

This year, let's first ask God to give us wisdom because He gives it to those who ask, then let's seek out Godly counsel when we need advice. Everyone cannot advise you in your journey to your destiny!

Proverbs 3:7; Proverbs 19:20; Proverbs 16:25

May 4

Daily Devotion for DESTINY:

John 4:23 (English Standard Version) - **23** But the hour is coming, and is now here, when the true worshipers will worship the Father in spirit and truth, for the Father is seeking such people to worship him.

It is Thankful Day! One sign of a thankful heart is the ability to worship God in Spirit and Truth. The scripture says that He is seeking such to worship Him. This lets us know that there is not an overabundance of people actually worshipping God in Spirit and in Truth. If there were, He would not have to seek for such.

John MacArthur in his book "The Ultimate Priority" gives a simple definition of worship: "Worship is all that we are responding correctly to all that He is." Since God is love, we respond to His love by walking in love.

Let's make this year the year that we purify our worship by walking in love. This is a result of a thankful heart.

John 5:25; Galatians 4:6; Isaiah 29:13

May 5

Daily Devotion for DESTINY:

Hebrews 11:8-9 (English Standard Version) –
8 By faith Abraham obeyed when he was called to go out to a place that he was to receive as an inheritance. And he went out, not knowing where he was going. **9** By faith he went to live in the land of promise, as in a foreign land, living in tents with Isaac and Jacob, heirs with him of the same promise

Happy Faith Day! Hebrews 11 is often referred to as the "Hall of Faith" because it outlines the faith walk of many of the generals of faith. One of my favorites is Abraham. He was 75 years old when he set out to obey God in search of a land that would someday be his inheritance.

Abraham did not start out with great faith. He meditated on the word of God to build his faith and built an altar to talk to God every chance he got. In doing so, he learned to distinguish the voice of God from all of the other voices that speaks to us.

What is God challenging you to believe Him for? If He is challenging you to believe Him for something, it is because that is what He wants to do for you and He needs your faith to bring it to pass. You are never too old to believe God!

Genesis 12:1-4; Genesis 12:7; Isaiah 51:12

May 6

Daily Devotion for DESTINY:

Isaiah 55:6 (English Standard Version) - "Seek the Lord while he may be found; call upon him while he is near

Our scripture today is admonishing us to seek the Lord while He may be found. This implies that there is a time coming when He cannot be found.

We seek God to get to know His will. Reaching our destiny and obtaining the promises of God requires our participation. We must meditate on God's word, transform our minds, ask God for wisdom, be thankful to Him and walk by faith!

Starting today and every day, let's set aside some time to seek the Lord. If you do this, I assure you that you will find Him!

Jeremiah 29:12-13; Amos 5:6; Psalms 14:2

May 7

Daily Devotion for DESTINY:

Jeremiah 17:7-8 (New International Version) - **7** "But blessed is the one who trusts in the Lord whose confidence is in him. **8They** will be like a tree planted by the water that sends out its roots by the stream. It does not fear when heat comes; its leaves are always green. It has no worries in a year of drought and never fails to bear fruit."

It is very easy to get shaken up when we get bad news, or when we see what is happening in the world. Our scripture today reminds us that no matter what is happening around us, if we put our trust in God, we will not be moved. We will be like a tree planted by the water.

The Water (Holy Spirit) will keep our roots (faith) watered so that when the heat (trials & tribulations) come, we will not fear. Because of the water (Holy Spirit), our leaves are green and we will bear fruit even during the drought.

This year, let's be sure that our roots (faith) is deeply planted by the Water (Holy Spirit) so that we can bear fruit in spite of the drought.

Isaiah 26:3-4; Psalms 34:8; Proverbs 16:20

May 8

Daily Devotion for DESTINY:

Psalms 32:8 (New International Version) - **8** I will instruct you and teach you in the way you should go;I will counsel you with my loving eye on you.

Happy Meditation Day! This is the time of year of uncertainty for many people. Maybe you are graduating for High School or College, or maybe you are just entering a new season in your life and are not sure where to go from here.

Whatever season you are in, I want to encourage you to consult the Lord for your next move. Meditate on our scripture for today and allow God to speak direction to your heart.

Let us make this season successful by acknowledging God in all our ways and allowing Him to direct our paths!

Proverbs 3:5-6; Psalms 33:18; Matthew 11:29

May 9

Daily Devotion for DESTINY:

Philippians 1:6 (The Amplified Bible, classic edition) - **6** And I am convinced *and* sure of this very thing, that He Who began a good work in you will continue until the day of Jesus Christ [right up to the time of His return], developing [that good work] *and* perfecting *and* bringing it to full completion in you.

It is Transformation Day! From the time that we accept Jesus as Lord and Savior of our lives, the transformation begins. Our spirits are transformed immediately, but we have to transform our minds to agree with our new spirit. We do this by meditating on the word of God.

We are not alone in this transformation. Jesus began the good work in us when He came to live in our hearts (spirit). He will continue this work until the day that He comes back for us.

This year, let's allow Jesus to perfect His work in us and complete our transformation.

Philippians 2:13; Ephesians 4:12; Psalms 138:8

May 10

Daily Devotion for DESTINY:

Proverbs 19:8 (The Amplified Bible, classic edition) - **8** He who gains Wisdom loves his own life; he who keeps understanding shall prosper *and* find good.

It is Wisdom Day! We have learned that if we want wisdom, that we should ask God who will give it to all who ask for it. God gives us wisdom by speaking instructions and directions to our hearts.

Our scripture today tells us that if we love our own life, we will do what it takes to get and maintain wisdom. Once you have gained it, make sure that you keep it. If we hang on to the wisdom that we have attained, we will be happy now and forever.

This year, let's take responsibility for our own happiness by first getting, then maintaining wisdom.

I Peter 3:10; Proverbs 17:16; Proverbs 4:6

May 11

Daily Devotion for DESTINY:

Colossians 4:2 (The Amplified Bible, classic edition) - **2** Be earnest *and* unwearied *and* steadfast in your prayer [life], being [both] alert *and* intent in [your praying] with thanksgiving.

Welcome to Thankful Day! One thing that is very clear from our scripture today is that it is God's will that we pray. Thanking God should always be a part of our prayers. They are the power couple!

When we mix thanksgiving with our prayers, it shows God that we believe that we will receive what we asked because we are asking according to His will for our lives.

This year, let's devote ourselves to prayer with Thanksgiving. This will link us to the will of God for us!

I Thessalonians 5:17-18; Philippians 4:6; Luke 18:1

May 12

Daily Devotion for DESTINY:

II Timothy 4:7 (The Amplified Bible, classic edition) - **7** I have fought the good (worthy, honorable, and noble) fight, I have finished the race, I have kept (firmly held) the faith.

Happy Faith Day! Becoming a Christian is fairly easy. You confess with your mouth the Lord Jesus and believe in your heart that God has raised Him from the dead, and the bible says that you are saved!

Then comes the hard part. Hanging onto (and growing) the faith that it took to get saved. From that moment on, it becomes satan's mission to steal your faith. Even he knows that without faith it is impossible to please God.

Let's be determined this year to not only hang on to our faith but continue to grow it. Then at the end of our lives, we can say that we have fought the good fight and we won!

I Timothy 6:12; Acts 20:24; John 17:6

May 13

Daily Devotion for DESTINY:

Proverbs 4:25-27 (The Amplified Bible, classic edition) - 25 Let your eyes look right on [with fixed purpose], and let your gaze be straight before you. 26 Consider well the path of your feet and let all your ways be established and ordered aright. 27 Turn not aside to the right hand or to the left; remove your foot from evil.

Our scripture for today is the recipe for success if your goal is to move forward in the things of God. Looking straight ahead signifies your intent to move from one dimension to the next. It is satan's job to put distractions in your path and hope that you lose your focus.

We must be determined to keep our eyes gazing straight ahead of us and ponder (meditate using the word of God) the path of our feet. Whatever we do, we must not swerve to the right or left and we must make sure we turn our foot from evil.

This year, if we use this recipe for success, we will end up at our destination with nothing missing and nothing broken.

Matthew 6:22; Psalms 119:37; Proverbs 23:5

May 14

Daily Devotion for DESTINY:

Titus 2:3-5 (English Standard Version) - **3** Older women likewise are to be reverent in behavior, not slanderers or slaves to much wine. They are to teach what is good, **4** and so train the young women to love their husbands and children, **5** to be self-controlled, pure, working at home, kind, and submissive to their own husbands, that the word of God may not be reviled.

I think that our scripture today is very befitting. Many older women are falling away from the teaching of the scriptures; therefore, the younger women are losing their way.

We as older (and hopefully wiser) women must teach younger women how to be (amongst many other things) successful mothers. We wear many different hats. Whether we work outside of the home, or we work as a stay-at-home mom, we are the example of what God had in mind when he created mothers.

This year, let's focus on being an example of a Godly mother and making a clear path for our daughters and nieces to follow.

I Timothy 3:11; Romans 16:1-2; Hebrews 5:12

May 15

Daily Devotion for DESTINY:

Proverbs 15:28 (The Amplified Bible, classic edition) - **28** The mind of the [uncompromisingly] righteous studies how to answer, but the mouth of the wicked pours out evil things.

It is Meditation Day! The bible encourages meditating on the word of God because it adds insight and understanding not only to our speech, but also to our behavior.

Meditation is not something that can be done in a hurry. It requires focus and concentration. It is very important to set aside uninterrupted time with God every day. If you do, He will meet you there and reward you openly because you sought Him in private.

This year, let's add to our time with God. If you normally give Him 15 minutes, give Him 30 minutes. I promise you that you won't be disappointed.

James 3:6-8; Matthew 12:34; Ecclesiastes 5:2

May 16

Daily Devotion for DESTINY:

James 1:2-4 (English Standard Version) - **2** Count it all joy, my brothers,[a] when you meet trials of various kinds, **3** for you know that the testing of your faith produces steadfastness. **4** And let steadfastness have its full effect, that you may be perfect and complete, lacking in nothing.

It is Transformation Day! A huge part of our transformation comes through our trials and tribulations. During the times when our faith is being tested, we must make sure that patience is being perfected in us.

Our scripture today is telling us to count it as joy when our faith is being tested because once our patience is perfected and our faith has grown, we develop a disciplined obedience to Christ.

This year, let's allow the trying of our faith to transform us into fully developed Christians whose joy is not dependent on circumstances, but on our faith in Christ!

James 1:12; Romans 8:17-18; Philippians 1:29

May 17

Daily Devotion for DESTINY:

Isaiah 5:21 (The Amplified Bible, classic edition) - **21** Woe to those who are wise in their own eyes and prudent *and* shrewd in their own sight!

Happy Wisdom Day! Our scripture today is a warning to those who has an inflated opinion of their own wisdom and knowledge and who are overly confident and vain.

James 3:17 tells us the characteristics of the wisdom that comes from God. It is pure, peaceable, gentle, open to reason, full of mercy and good fruits, impartial and sincere. If the characteristics of your wisdom is anything other than the above, it didn't come from God!

This year, let's strive to attain the wisdom that comes from God. The bible said that if we lack this wisdom, just ask God. In doing so, we will save ourselves and others.

Proverbs 3:7; I Corinthians 3:18-20; Romans 12:6

May 18

Daily Devotion for DESTINY:

II Corinthians 9:15 (The Amplified Bible, classic edition) - **15** Now thanks be to God for His Gift, [precious] beyond telling [His indescribable, inexpressible, free Gift]!

It is Thankful Day! Our scripture today leaves us to ponder what gift the Apostle is referring to. Is it the love of God as manifested in Christ? Is it the gift of the Holy Spirit, or is it the gift of forgiveness of our sins?

When we think on any of these gifts, it puts us in the Thanksgiving mode. What gift has God given you just this week that you are thankful for?

Today, let's put aside our cares and worries. Let's make a conscious decision to replace worry with thanksgiving to God for all of the gifts that He has given us not only this week, but throughout our lives!

Ephesians 5:20; I Corinthians 15:57; Psalms 30:4

May 19

Daily Devotion for DESTINY:

I Timothy 4:12 (The Amplified Bible, classic edition) - **12** Let no one despise *or* think less of you because of your youth but be an example (pattern) for the believers in speech, in conduct, in love, in faith, and in purity.

Happy Faith Day! In our scripture today, Paul is encouraging Timothy as a young man to be an example in speech, conduct, love, faith and purity.

Young people today are looking for examples. Someone that they feel can relate to their struggles and at the same time, guide them to the one that can relieve their struggles. It is important that the young people that have made Jesus the Lord of their lives be that example for those that are searching.

Let's make this the year that we as Christians (whether young or old) be an example in speech, conduct, purity and particularly in faith!

Titus 2:7; II Timothy 2:22; I Corinthians

May 20

Daily Devotion for DESTINY:

I Peter 4:12 (The Amplified Bible, classic edition) - **12** Beloved, do not be amazed *and* bewildered at the fiery ordeal which is taking place to test your quality, as though something strange (unusual and alien to you and your position) were befalling you.

When we read our scripture today, we understand that doing God's will is not a guarantee that we will escape suffering. As a matter of fact, the opposite is true. Doing God's will is a guarantee that our faith will be tested.

We must not think it strange if we suffer on our journey towards our destiny. In this case, we are suffering within God's will.

This year, let's press on towards our destiny and prepare ourselves for the trials that we will encounter on the way. Most importantly, we must not become weary in well doing, for we shall reap if we faint not!

I Peter 5:9; II Timothy 3:12; I Peter 1:6-7

May 21

Daily Devotion for DESTINY:

Numbers 23:19 (The Amplified Bible, classic edition) - **19** God is not a man, that He should tell *or* act a lie, neither the son of man, that He should feel repentance *or* compunction [for what He has promised]. Has He said and shall He not do it? Or has He spoken and shall He not make it good?

I heard this scripture so clearly in my spirit this morning. Please know that as your faith is being tested that God CANNOT lie! If He said it, you can believe that it will surely come to pass!

Do not be moved by what you see or feel. We must only be moved by the word of God! Sometimes when we are going through trials and tribulations, we begin to doubt God and His promises to us. This doubt limits what God is able to do for us.

This year, let's get into the word of God to find out what He promised us then agree with Him. Once you do this, you will agree that God CANNOT lie, and you will see each and every promise come to pass!!

Luke 21:33; Habakkuk 2:3; Titus 1:2

May 22

Daily Devotion for DESTINY:

II Corinthians 10:4-5 (New King James Version) -4 For the weapons of our warfare *are* not carnal but mighty in God for pulling down strongholds, **5** casting down arguments and every high thing that exalts itself against the knowledge of God, bringing every thought into captivity to the obedience of Christ,

Good morning! It is Meditation Day! Since meditation takes place in our minds and begins with our thoughts, it is important to understand how to keep our focus while we meditate.

During the course of life, we develop strongholds in our minds. Strongholds are incorrect thinking patterns that have molded itself into our way of thinking. As we renew our minds by meditating on the word of God, we can destroy the strongholds that are in our minds and cast away every thought that exalts itself against the knowledge of God.

Make this the year that we bring every thought into captivity to the obedience of Christ. You will be glad that you did!

Romans 7:23; Hebrews 4:12; Romans 1:21

May 23

Daily Devotion for DESTINY:

II Corinthians 3:18 (English Standard Version) – [18] And we all, with unveiled face, beholding the glory of the Lord,[a] are being transformed into the same image from one degree of glory to another.[b] For this comes from the Lord who is the Spirit.

It is Transformation Day! In our scripture today, Paul wanted to emphasize the freedom that we have as Christians. He does this by referencing the veil that Moses wore when he talked to God.

We come before the Lord with unveiled faces. The glory that we encounter when we approach God transforms us into His likeness. God is making our inner thoughts, character and our attitudes like His own.

This year, let's allow the Holy Spirit to continue the work of transforming us into His image and into His likeness.

Romans 12:2; I Corinthians 13:12; I Corinthians 15:49

May 24

Daily Devotion for DESTINY:

Psalms 90:12 (English Standard Version) - So teach us to number our days that we may get a heart of wisdom.

Welcome to Wisdom Day! God sees and knows the time and manner when life will end for us. Even though in most instances this information is hidden from us, He desires for us to act as if we know as well.

A wise person would make the most out of their lives and would have different objectives if they knew exactly when their life would end.

This year (and every year forward) let's be wise and live our lives as if every day will be our last!

Psalms 39:4; Ephesians 5:16-17; John 9:4

May 25

Daily Devotion for DESTINY:

Psalms 92:1-2 (English Standard Version) -
It is good to give thanks to the Lord,
to sing praises to your name, O Most High;
2 to declare your steadfast love in the morning,
and your faithfulness by night,

It is Thankful Day! The theme of Thanksgiving is woven all throughout the scriptures. A day that begins and ends with praise and thanksgiving will always be a great day!

Praise and thanksgiving is a good barometer of our spiritual health. If our praise and thanksgiving are on point, our daily victories will be the norm. Thanksgiving will not end when heaven begins. That is what we will be doing in eternity.

This year, let's heighten our thanksgiving and praise to God because He has certainly heightened His goodness towards us.

Ephesians 5:19; Psalms 125:3; Psalms 107:1

May 26

Daily Devotion for DESTINY:

Isaiah 40:31 (The Amplified Bible, classic edition) - **31** But those who wait for the Lord [who expect, look for, and hope in Him] shall change *and* renew their strength *and* power; they shall lift their wings *and* mount up [close to God] as eagles [mount up to the sun]; they shall run and not be weary, they shall walk and not faint *or* become tired.

Happy Faith Day! The waiting in our scripture today refers to the expectant attitude of faith that we have as Christians. Just as the eagle's wings are renewed in their old age, so are we renewed when our faith is in God!

God has begun a work in us. When we put our faith in Him, He will complete what He started. There is no failure for the faithful. We will not grow weary because we hope in Him.

This year, let's determine that we will not give in to the pressures of life because our trust (faith) is in God!

II Corinthians 4:16; Psalms 27:13-14; Galatians 6:9

May 27

Daily Devotion for DESTINY:

Matthew 5:13-14 (The Amplified Bible, classic edition) - **13** You are the salt of the earth, but if salt has lost its taste (its strength, its quality), how can its saltiness be restored? It is not good for anything any longer but to be thrown out and trodden underfoot by men.**14** You are the light of the world. A city set on a hill cannot be hidden.

I saw a meme on Facebook that has been in my spirit ever since I read it. It said, "Become who you needed when you were younger". Many of our young people are leaving here without knowing that God made them for a specific purpose and that He gave them a destiny that only they can fulfill.

Our scripture today tells us that we as Christians are the seasoning (salt) of the earth. Salt is a preservative. We are the light for our young people and for the world. In a world that is so dark, our children need a light to know where they should go. Once we have found our way in this world, it is our assignment to light the path for the ones that will come after us.

This year, let's focus on becoming the light that we needed when we were younger and light the path for those assigned to our lives to follow us!

Colossians 4:6; Luke 14:34-34; Leviticus 2:13

May 28

Daily Devotion for DESTINY:

Isaiah 55:10-11 (English Standard Version) - "For as the rain and the snow come down from heaven and do not return there but water the earth, making it bring forth and sprout, giving seed to the sower and bread to the eater, **11** so shall my word be that goes out from my mouth; it shall not return to me empty, but it shall accomplish that which I purpose, and shall succeed in the thing for which I sent it.

One of the assignments of a Prophet is to speak life into a dying situation. This is precisely what the prophet Isaiah is speaking to the exiles of Babylonian captivity. The trauma of what they had lived through seemed too much to bear.

The Prophet likened the Word of God to rain and snow. The rain comes down to water the seeds in the earth and does not return until it has completed this task that is necessary for a harvest.

Are you going through a trauma today The Word of God is available to water the seeds that God planted in you at birth and the Word will not return until it has accomplished what God intended for it to accomplish in your life.

This year, let's make the Word of God our own. It will water the seeds that God planted in us. In doing so, we can transform the earth!

Isaiah 30:23; Deuteronomy 32:2; Revelation 11:6

May 29

Daily Devotion for DESTINY:

I John 3:16 (The Amplified Bible, classic edition) -**16** By this we come to know (progressively to recognize, to perceive, to understand) the [essential] love: that He laid down His [own] life for us; and we ought to lay [our] lives down for [those who are our] brothers [[a]in Him].

Happy Meditation Day!Today, let's remember our heroes that have given their lives for our freedom, Let us remember the very first hero that gave His life for our freedom from sin.

Jesus made it possible for us to lay down our lives (some literally) for our brothers and sisters by first laying down His life for us. We know that Jesus loves us because He laid down His life for us.

Today, as we meditate on and honor the men and women that have given their lives for us; Let us reflect on the love that it must have taken to do such a selfless act; then let's pay it forward!

Romans 5:8; I John 4:9-10; Romans 8:32

May 30

Daily Devotion for DESTINY:

Matthew 16:15-17 (English Standard Version) - **15** He said to them, "But who do you say that I am?" **16** Simon Peter replied, "You are the Christ, the Son of the living God." **17** And Jesus answered him, "Blessed are you, Simon Bar-Jonah! For flesh and blood has not revealed this to you, but my Father who is in heaven.

It is Transformation Day! The Word of God is necessary in our pursuit of transforming our minds. What is just as important is allowing the Holy Spirit to reveal the meaning of the Word to our spirits. This is called "revelation knowledge"

In our scripture today, the Holy Spirit revealed the identity of Jesus to Simon Peter before it became common knowledge that He is the Messiah! We must allow the Holy Spirit to give us the revelation of the Word of God and the wisdom of how to apply it to our lives each day.

This year, let's meditate on God's word and seek Him for the revelation of His Word. Revelation gives birth to Transformation!

John 11:27;Matthew 14:33; Acts 9:20

May 31

Daily Devotion for DESTINY:

Proverbs 9:10 (The Amplified Bible, classic edition) - **10** The reverent *and* worshipful fear of the Lord is the beginning (the chief and choice part) of Wisdom, and the knowledge of the Holy One is insight *and* understanding.

Welcome to Wisdom Day! Our scripture today shows where true wisdom begins. The person that fears the Lord is wise. It is important to note that "fear" in this context means "to stand in awe of. It is the reverence that you feel when you are in the presence of greatness!

To put it simply, wisdom is seeing life from God's perspective and responding accordingly. Our minds must be filled with the knowledge of God and His way of doing things.

This year, let's focus on the Kingdom of God and His way of doing things. When we do, we cannot help but to stand in awe of Him!

Proverbs 1:7; Psalms 111:10; Job 28:28

June

2 Do not
conform to
the pattern
of this
world but
be
transformed
by the
renewing
of your
mind. Then
you will be
able to test
and
approve
what God's
will is—his
good,
pleasing
and perfect
will.

Romans 12:2 (NIV)

June 1

Daily Devotion for DESTINY:

John 10:10 (The Amplified Bible, classic edition) - **10** The thief comes only in order to steal and kill and destroy. I came that they may have *and* enjoy life, and have it in abundance (to the full, till it [a]overflows).

It is Thankful Day! Every time I read our scripture for today, it puts me in thanksgiving mode. Just think about the fact that the thief (satan) came to steal, kill and destroy us; but God came to give us not just life but abundant life!

In other words, God will not allow satan to fulfill his purpose in our lives. God has our back when we make decisions that leads to life and not death! Are you thankful for that?

This year, let's focus on living the abundant life that God ordained for us and be full of thanksgiving in the process!

Luke 19:10; John 3:17; Matthew 20:28

June 2

Daily Devotion for DESTINY:

Matthew 15:28 (English Standard Version) - **28** Then Jesus answered her, "O woman, great is your faith! Be it done for you as you desire." And her daughter was healed instantly.[a]

Happy Faith Day! I want to point out how important it is for parents to have faith not only for themselves, but for their children as well. We must be the example of walking by faith and not by sight because our children are certainly watching.

In Deuteronomy, the Jewish people were told to have no dealings with the Canaanites. When this Canaanite mother came to Jesus begging for deliverance for her daughter, Jesus broke all of the rules for her because her faith was great!

This year, let's be an example of great faith to our children and allow Jesus to break all of the rules for us and for them!

Mark 5:34; Matthew 9:22; Matthew 8:10

June 3

Daily Devotion for DESTINY

John 16:3 (English Standard Version) - **13** When the Spirit of truth comes, he will guide you into all the truth, for he will not speak on his own authority, but whatever he hears he will speak, and he will declare to you the things that are to come.

Christ's departure from this earth was necessary in order for the Holy Spirit to come. Jesus' human body could only be in one place at one time, but His Spirit is everywhere at all times.

A part of the Holy Spirit's work is to convince us that we are in sin and have need of a Savior. He lets us know that Jesus is that Savior. This is the truth that the Holy Spirit guides us to.

Today, if you need a Savior, allow the Holy Spirit to lead you to Jesus and put you on the path to your destiny!

John 15:26; John 14:17; I John 4:6

June 4

Daily Devotion for DESTINY:

Proverbs 12:25 (The Amplified Bible, classic edition) - **25** Anxiety in a man's heart weighs it down, but an encouraging word makes it glad.

Are you anxious this morning? Is your heart heavy? The scripture says that an encouraging word will make your heart glad.

If you can make your way to a bible-believing church on this Pentecost Day and allow the Holy Spirit to give us a word in due season, you will make it!

This morning, let's replace our spirit of heaviness with a garment of praise and continue our God-ordained path towards our destiny!

Isaiah 50:4; Proverbs 15:23; Proverbs 17:22

June 5

Daily Devotion for DESTINY:

Psalms 119:97 (The Amplified Bible, classic edition) - **97** Oh, how love I Your law! It is my meditation all day.

Happy Meditation Day! Meditation is a God-ordained way to study the scriptures. In our scripture today, David states that he loves and meditates on the law of the Lord. I have to believe that this is one of the many reasons that he was a man after God's own heart (Acts 13:22).

We are living in a day and time where the Word (law) of God is not given much attention. This can be changed when we as Christians develop a passion and longing for the Word of God. It is contagious!

Let's make this the year that we meditate on the Word of God until we have developed such a longing for it that we need it daily!

Psalms 1:2; Deuteronomy 17:19; Joshua 1:8

June 6

Daily Devotion for DESTINY:

II Timothy 2:15 (King James Version) - **15** Study to shew thyself approved unto God, a workman that needeth not to be ashamed, rightly dividing the word of truth.

It is Transformation Day! A major part of our transformation is studying (meditating) on the Word of God. The Word of God changes us from the inside out. We are not studying to be approved by men. We are studying to be approved by God.

We as Christians are all representatives of God. It is important that we rightly divide (interpret) His word so that we do not make Him ashamed. It is just as important that we allow the word to transform us to the point that when people encounter us, they feel as if they have had an encounter with the Lord.

This year, let's study (meditate) on the word so that our lives resemble the Word of God. This is a transformed life!

II Peter 1:10; II Corinthians 10:18; Galatians 1:10

June 7

Daily Devotion for DESTINY:

Proverbs 14:16 (English Standard Version) - One who is wise is cautious[a] and turns away from evil, but a fool is reckless and careless.

Wisdom Day is here! Our scripture today holds a few nuggets on the actions of a wise man/woman. When you are wise, you are very careful to abstain from even the appearance of sin.

A wise man/woman has such respect for the Lord that they avoid every opportunity to sin that comes their way. The scripture says that a fool is the opposite. They do not respect God nor His representatives. A fool has confidence in his own wisdom rather than the wisdom of God.

This year as we gain wisdom and understanding, let's make sure that it is the wisdom that comes from above and not our own wisdom.

Proverbs 3:7; I Thessalonians 5:22; Psalms 34:14

June 8

Daily Devotion for DESTINY:

Romans 2:4 (New King James Version) - **4** Or do you despise the riches of His goodness, forbearance, and longsuffering, not knowing that the goodness of God leads you to repentance?

Thankful Day has arrived! I am so thankful for the patience and long-suffering of God towards me. I think about all of the times I did the opposite of what He told me, and He still blessed me.

Our scripture today lets us know that the goodness of God is intended to lead us to repentance. We must not take His goodness as a sign that He is pleased with us.

Today, if you have been in a season where you have not been on the same page as God, thank Him for being patient and kind, then make every effort to get on the same page as He is on. God will then take His goodness to a whole new level! I am a witness!

II Peter 3:9; Romans 3:26; Isaiah 30:18

June 9

Daily Devotion for DESTINY:

Galatians 5:6 (The Amplified Bible, classic edition) - **6** For [if we are] in Christ Jesus, neither circumcision nor uncircumcision counts for anything, but only faith activated *and* energized *and expressed and* working through love.

Happy Faith Day! Our scripture today lets us know that our faith has a twin. It is love. We know that faith comes by hearing (with our heart) the word of God, but it is activated and energized by our love.

Dr. D L Moody said that "Faith makes all things possible, love makes all things easy." While we are building our faith by meditating on the Word of God, let's remember to build our love as well.

This year, lets focus on balancing our faith with our love so that we can see the promises of God come to pass in our lives.

I Thessalonians 1:3; Hebrews 11:8; I Timothy 1:5

June 10

Daily Devotion for DESTINY:

Proverbs 16:7 (The Amplified bible, classic edition) - **7** When a man's ways please the Lord, He makes even his enemies to be at peace with him.

The best way to be a peace with our enemies is to be at peace with our God. We are at peace with God when we walk after the Spirit not after the flesh and when we walk by faith not by sight.

Just as the King's heart was in the hand of the Lord, so are our hearts and according to Proverbs 21:1, God can turn our hearts whichever way He wills.

Do you have any foes today? Focus on pleasing the Lord, then enjoy the peace that follows.

Proverbs 21:1; Jeremiah 15:11; I John 3:22

June 11

Daily Devotion for DESTINY:

Galatians 1:15-16 (The Amplified Bible) - **15** But when God, who had chosen me *and* set me apart before I was born, and called me through His grace, was pleased **16** to reveal His Son in me so that I might preach Him among the Gentiles [as the good news—the way of salvation], I did not immediately consult with [a]anyone [for guidance regarding God's call and His revelation to me].

We are half-way through the year! Do you know what your purpose for being on this earth is yet? We have set aside this year to discover the reason that God created us and to begin our walk towards our destiny.

In our scripture today, the Apostle Paul said that when he discovered his purpose, he did not go immediately to consult with anyone about what God revealed to him about his purpose. Paul waited until God gave him permission to reveal his purpose and his assignment to the people.

Let's make the second half of this year the best half of this year! Meditate and transform your mind through the Word of God, Ask Him for wisdom, be thankful unto Him and increase your faith. If you do these things, you will not only discover your purpose, but you will be well on your way to your destination!

Jeremiah 1:5; Acts 9:15; Romans 1:1

June 12

Daily Devotion for DESTINY:

Psalms 1:2-3 (The Living Bible) - **2** But they delight in doing everything God wants them to, and day and night are always meditating on his laws and thinking about ways to follow him more closely.**3** They are like trees along a riverbank bearing luscious fruit each season without fail. Their leaves shall never wither, and all they do shall prosper.

Happy Meditation Day! There are blessing for us when we delight in pleasing God and when we meditate on the Word of God. We cannot find pleasure hanging out with those whose priority is not to please God.

We have God's approval when we seek to know Him better by meditating on His Word. God blesses what He approves. He will bless us so much that we will always bear fruit in our lives and everything we do shall prosper.

Do you want that blessing in your life this year? Seek to please the Lord and meditate on His Word and the blessings of the Lord will chase you down!

Jeremiah 17:8; Psalms 92:14; Genesis 39:3

June 13

Daily Devotion for DESTINY:

Ephesians 4:22-24 (English Standard Version) - **2** to put off your old self,[a] which belongs to your former manner of life and is corrupt through deceitful desires, **23** and to be renewed in the spirit of your minds, **24** and to put on the new self, created after the likeness of God in true righteousness and holiness.

Good morning! It is Transformation Day! Jesus changes our lives radically once we accept Him as Lord and Savior. We then spend a lifetime transforming into the image of God. This process begins by renewing our minds with the Word of God.

Renewing our mind brings our will into agreement with our Father's will. This results in a transformation of our entire being. It is God's will that we live victoriously in this life.

God provided a way for us to be transformed from the inside out. This year, let's begin the life-long process of transformation in our lives and live the life that God intended for us to live from the beginning of time.

Romans 6:6; James 1:21; Ephesians 4:17

June 14

Daily Devotion for DESTINY:

Proverbs 24:14 (The Amplified Bible, classic edition) - **14** So shall you know skillful *and* Godly Wisdom to be thus to your life; if you find it, then shall there be a future *and* a reward, and your hope *and expectation* shall not be cut off.

It is Wisdom Day! I want to encourage everyone to seek wisdom because it is both pleasurable and profitable. You will encounter some difficulties in the pursuit of wisdom, but you will enjoy the rewards for the rest of your life.

Since wisdom is valuable for our souls, it makes our efforts to obtain it a priority. There are several ways to obtain wisdom. We can ask God and we can read (meditate) on His Word each and every day. God offers wisdom freely, but He does not force it on us.

This year, let's seek to obtain and maintain wisdom. Its rewards will far outweigh the efforts to obtain it.

Proverbs 23:18; Proverbs 2:10; James 1:25

June 15

Daily Devotion for DESTINY:

Romans 5:1 (English Standard Version) - **5** Therefore, since we have been justified by faith, we[a] have peace with God through our Lord Jesus Christ.

It is Thankful Day! I am thankful today because I have peace with God through my Savior, Jesus Christ. I have this peace because I have been justified through my faith.

What this means is that when we accept Jesus as our Lord and Savior and begin to live our lives according to His word, He justifies us. Justification means JUST AS IF WE NEVER SINNED!!!

Are you thankful that you have been justified? If you are, give God a praise unlike any other.

Isaiah 32:17; Romans 6:23; Galatians 2:16

June 16

Daily Devotion for DESTINY:

John 7:38 (English Standard Version) - **38** Whoever believes in me, as[a] the Scripture has said, 'Out of his heart will flow rivers of living water.'"

Happy Faith Day! When we live in communion with God, He becomes the center of our universe. There is a power in Him that when quickened by faith, flows like a river into our lives.

The reference of the life-giving water is used often throughout the scriptures to describe the Holy Spirit. When we exercise our faith and allow the Holy Spirit to give us life, we become instrumental in refreshing and comforting others.

This year, let's believe God so much that we become that flow of living water that the world so desperately needs!

Isaiah 58:11; John 4:14; John 4:10

June 17

Daily Devotion for DESTINY:

I John 2:3-4 (English Standard Version) - And by this we know that we have come to know him, if we keep his commandments. **4** Whoever says "I know him" but does not keep his commandments is a liar, and the truth is not in him,

According to the Word of God, if we know God, we must keep His commandments. It is becoming more and more popular in this day and age to claim to know God, but still live our lives pleasing our flesh each and every day. The bible says that if we claim to know God but do not keep His commandments (both specific commands and principles), we are liars!

As we are discovering our purpose and walking towards our destiny, we must make sure that we are also laying aside every weight and sin that so easily besets us (Hebrews 12:1) and doing our best to follow God's commands. When we do this, our journey will be a lot lighter!

I john 1:6; I John 1:8; I John 1:10

June 18

Daily Devotion for DESTINY:

Matthew 7:9-11 (English Standard Version) - **9** Or which one of you, if his son asks him for bread, will give him a stone? **10** Or if he asks for a fish, will give him a serpent? **11** If you then, who are evil, know how to give good gifts to your children, how much more will your Father who is in heaven give good things to those who ask him!

There is something very special about fathers (like my own) who raised their children in the fear and admonition (awe and respect) of the Lord. Our earthly fathers are the first representatives of a father to us. They play a huge role in how we respond to our heavenly Father.

If you did not have an earthly father figure in your life, do not fret! You have been adopted into the royal family by Father God! Invite Him into your life. Being to meditate on His word to learn about Him. Talk to Him and listen as He talks to you.

Allow God to give good gifts to you just as your earthly fathers did. He will always be there for you and He will never let you down!

Romans 8:32; I John 4:10; Psalms 84:11

June 19

Daily Devotion for DESTINY:

Psalms 119:48 (English Standard Version) - I will lift up my hands toward your commandments, which I love, and I will meditate on your statutes.

Happy Meditation Day! We as Christians must prioritize the art of meditating on God's word. With technology today, we have many options to keep the Word of God with us constantly.

Our faith is renewed and we draw hope from meditating on God's word. God's word when meditated on and spoken in faith, transforms our lives on a daily basis.

Let's make this year the year that we draw from God's life-giving Spirit as we meditate on His word.

Psalms 1:2; Psalms 119:15; John 13:17

June 20

Daily Devotion for DESTINY

Galatians 5:22-23 (English Standard Version) - **22** But the fruit of the Spirit is love, joy, peace, patience, kindness, goodness, faithfulness, **23** gentleness, self-control; against such things there is no law.

It is Transformation Day! A transformed life involves walking in the Spirit versus walking in the flesh. Our scripture today shows us what our lives will look like when we begin to walk in the Spirit.

Notice that the word "Fruit" is singular. What this means is the "Fruit" of the Holy Spirit is LOVE and it manifests itself in joy, peace, patience, kindness, goodness, faithfulness, gentleness and self-control.

This year, let's grow in the Fruit of the Spirit (Love) and begin to live the transformed life that results from this decision. In doing so, we will transform the lives of our brothers and sisters.

John 15:5; Ephesians 5:9; Psalms 1:3

June 21

Daily Devotion for DESTINY:

Ecclesiastes 7:12 (New International Version) - Wisdom is a shelter as money is a shelter,

but the advantage of knowledge is this: Wisdom preserves those who have it.

Wisdom Day is here! Wisdom is an inheritance. It can (and should) be passed down from generation to generation. Wealth does not lengthen our lives. Wisdom can not only lengthen, but it will also strengthen our lives.

Once wisdom attained, it cannot be lost as money can. This makes wisdom even more valuable than money. Wisdom that comes from above gives life to those that find it.

Let's make this year the year that we enrich our lives by growing in wisdom.

Proverbs 3:18; Proverbs 8:35; Proverbs 2:7

June 22

Daily Devotion for DESTINY:

Hebrews 12:28-29 (English Standard Version) - **8** Therefore let us be grateful for receiving a kingdom that cannot be shaken, and thus let us offer to God acceptable worship, with reverence and awe, **29** for our God is a consuming fire.

Welcome to Thankful Day! Romans 14:17 tells us that the Kingdom of God is not meat and drink, but righteousness, peach and joy in the Holy Ghost. Our scripture today tells us that this Kingdom cannot be shaken and we should offer God "acceptable" worship.

The fact that the scriptures say that we should offer "acceptable" worship lets us know that there is a such thing as "unacceptable" worship. When we worship God in Spirit and in Truth, He becomes the consuming fire against our enemies.

This year, let's upgrade our worship so that it is acceptable to God and allow Him to consume our enemies.

Hebrews 5:7; Hebrews 4:16; Hebrews 10:27

June 23

Daily Devotion for DESTINY:

Galatians 2:16 (New International Version)- **16** know that a person is not justified by the works of the law, but by faith in Jesus Christ. So we, too, have put our faith in Christ Jesus that we may be justified by faith in[a] Christ and not by the works of the law, because by the works of the law no one will be justified.

Happy Faith Day! We as Christians have been justified (made free from guilt therefore from punishment in the sight of the Lord) and made righteous by our faith in Jesus. This status could not be attained by the works of the law.

During the era of Abraham, righteousness was based on the promise and his faith in the promise. Abraham believed God and it was counted unto him as righteousness (Galatians 3:6). Those of us who live in this era gain righteousness by faith in God.

This year, let's continue to build our faith so that we become righteous in the sight of the only one that matters: God!

Philippians 3:9; Romans 9:30; II Peter 1:1

June 24

Daily Devotion for DESTINY:

Luke 9:23 (English Standard Version) -**23** And he said to all, "If anyone would come after me, let him deny himself and take up his cross daily and follow me.

Our scripture today takes place immediately after Peter received the revelation that Jesus is the Messiah! Jesus told them not to reveal this revelation at that time because it was not yet time for His purpose to be revealed. There were still some things that He had to go through on the way to His destiny.

So it is with us. When we decide to follow Jesus, we must first deny our wants and desires and take up our cross DAILY. This means that we make decisions on a daily basis that will lead us through our trials and tribulations to our destination.

Let's make this year the year that we take up our cross and follow Jesus all the way to our destination. He knows the way!

Matthew 10:38-39; Romans 8:13; John 12:25-26

June 25

Daily Devotion for DESTINY:

John 17:17-18 (The Message Bible) - Make them holy—consecrated—with the truth; Your word is consecrating truth.In the same way that you gave me a mission in the world, I give them a mission in the world.

Our scripture today is part of one of Jesus' prayer for us (His followers). God has given us an assignment in life. The same assignment that God gave Jesus, He now gives to us. The assignment is to bring others into the saving knowledge of Jesus Christ. We are to build up the body.

God has given each of us our own unique purpose to accomplish this task. It is the reason that we are on this earth. Have you discovered your assignment? When we know God's reason for creating us, we can come into agreement with Him.

This year, let's discover our assignment and build the body of Christ!

II Corinthians 5:20; John 20:21; Ephesians 3:7

June 26

Daily Devotion for DESTINY:

Psalms 143:5 (English Standard Version) - I remember the days of old; I meditate on all that you have done; I ponder the work of your hands.

Happy Meditation Day! The purpose of biblical meditation is to empty the mind of all of the wrong mindsets that we developed prior to accepting Jesus into our lives and filling our minds with the Word of God. By meditating on God's word and the things that He has done for us in the past, we develop His mindset.

Biblical meditation allows God to speak to our hears as we reflect on His word. As we meditate, our thoughts are filtered by the Word of God; therefore, our thoughts become pure.

This year, let's take our meditation on God's word to a whole new level and allow His word to affect how we think, our attitudes and how we live our lives.

Psalms 111:4; Deuteronomy 8:2-3; Psalms 77:10-12

June 27

Daily Devotion for DESTINY:

Galatians 2:20 (English Standard Version) - **20** I have been crucified with Christ. It is no longer I who live, but Christ who lives in me. And the life I now live in the flesh I live by faith in the Son of God, who loved me and gave himself for me.

It is Transformation Day! We have been crucified with Christ! The law could not make man righteous before God. We were made righteous by Christ's death and resurrection. Romans 8:3 tells us that Christ did what the law could not do because it was too weak.

Jesus became an offering for sin so that we could become righteous before God. He made it possible for us to live our lives in the Spirit and not according to our flesh. This is a transformed life!

This year, let's continue to transform our lives by crucifying our flesh daily and living our lives by faith.

Romans 8:3; Galatians 5:24; II Corinthians 5:15

June 28

Daily Devotion for DESTINY:

Proverbs 19:20 (English Standard Version) - Listen to advice and accept instruction, that you may gain wisdom in the future.

Wisdom Day is upon us! Are we wiser today than we were last year? Our scripture today admonishes the young and old alike to be willing to receive counsel and instructions, particularly from the Word of God. In doing so, we will gain wisdom for our future.

Children of God should have a desire to grow in wisdom. We learned earlier that if we lack wisdom, we can ask God and He will gladly give it to us in abundance (James 1:5).

Today is our opportunity to change our latter end. Will we become wiser as we grow older? This year, choose wisdom!

Proverbs 12:15; Proverbs 1:8; Proverbs 4:1

June 29

Daily Devotion for DESTINY:

Psalms 92:1-2 (English Standard Version) - It is good to give thanks to the Lord, to sing praises to your name, O Most High; **2** to declare your steadfast love in the morning, and your faithfulness by night,

It is Thankful Day! Have you been dissed lately...disappointed, discouraged or disillusioned? This is a good time to give thanks the the Lord. Sing praises to His name because His love is steadfast!

The more intense the disappointment, disillusion or discouragement is, the more intense our thankfulness to God must be. As we begin to praise God in whatever circumstance we are in, we will find that even if the circumstance does not change, our attitude towards the circumstance changes from an attitude of defeat to an attitude of victory!

This year, let's intensify our gratitude towards God and watch our circumstances change!

Ephesians 5:19; Hebrews 13:15; Psalms 52:9

June 30

Daily Devotion for DESTINY:

Matthew 9:27-29 (English Standard Version) - **27** And as Jesus passed on from there, two blind men followed him, crying aloud, "Have mercy on us, Son of David." **28** When he entered the house, the blind men came to him, and Jesus said to them, "Do you believe that I am able to do this?" They said to him, "Yes, Lord." **29** Then he touched their eyes saying, "According to your faith be it done to you."

Happy Faith Day! How is our faith? Has it grown in the past 6 months? It is very important that we grow our faith. Our lives depend on it.

In our scripture today, two blind men came to Jesus and asked Him to have mercy (heal) on them. The first thing Jesus did was checked their faith. Once they confirmed that they believed that He could heal them, He told them that they would have what they believed.

These men walked away with their sight because they believed that Jesus could heal them. Let's build our faith this year so that we can have what the bible says that we can have!

Mark 9:23-24; John 11:40; Matthew 9:22

July

He carries out his decree against me,
and many such plans he still has in store.

Job 23:14 (NIV)

July 1

Daily Devotion for DESTINY:

Romans 8:28 (The Amplified Bible, classic edition) - **28** We are assured *and* know that [[a]God being a partner in their labor] all things work together *and* are [fitting into a plan] for good to *and* for those who love God and are called according to [His] design *and purpose.*

Each one of us has been born with a purpose and calling that we can either discover or completely miss. Our purpose must always be in the forefront of our minds. The influence of the Holy Spirit in our lives gives us insight into our purpose.

God's purpose for our lives can be fulfilled through multiple generations; therefore, it is important that we teach our children that they were born with an assignment. Their assignment may very well be an extension of your assignment.

Let's make this year the year that we not only discover our purpose and begin to walk in it, but we help our children discover their purpose. You will find that once you do this, all things will work together for your good!

I Corinthians 2:9; Romans 8:30; II Timothy 1:9

July 2

Daily Devotion for DESTINY:

Proverbs 19:21 (New International Version) - Many are the plans in a person's heart, but it is the Lord's purpose that prevails.

The Lord and His purposes are perfect, but we are not. We often have doubts and fears that hinders us from living out the purpose that God has established for us.

We often make plans and set out to accomplish them, but if we don't seek God's direction first; we really are not accomplishing anything. Every plan that we make for our lives should begin and end with God in mind.

This year, let's make great strides towards the plans and purposes that God has for us. We must keep in mind that our purpose is not only for us, but also for those assigned to us.

Proverbs 16:19; Isaiah 14:24; Ephesians 1:11

July 3

Daily Devotion for DESTINY:

Psalms 119:11 (New International Version) - I have hidden your word in my heart that I might not sin against you.

It's Meditation Day! When we meditate on the Word of God, it settles in our hearts. All of the word that we have read, heard preached or had revealed to us by the Holy Spirit becomes a part of our hearts when we meditate on them.

We hide the Word in our hearts so that we do not sin against God. This includes not only outward, fleshly sins (which we think of most often), but more importantly sins of the heart. These include (but are not limited to) unforgiveness, jealousy, envy, strife, etc.

This year, let's meditate and hide the Word of God in our hearts so that it will manifest in our lives.

Psalms 37:31; Colossians 3:16; Job 22:22

July 4

Daily Devotion for DESTINY:

Psalms 51:10 (English Standard Version) - Create in me a clean heart, O God, and renew a right[a] spirit within me.

Happy Transformation Day! True transformation and true independence starts in the heart. It is an inside job! We learned yesterday that if we hide the Word of God in our hearts, we will not sin against Him.

David asked God to create in Him a clean heart. It is no wonders that the bible describes David as "A man after God's own heart". God loves a clean heart because He knows that we will never gain true independence until we have a clean heart.

This year, let's allow God to transform us by creating a clean heart within us. As we meditate on the word, the Holy Spirit will cleanse our hearts from all unrighteousness and we will experience true independence in Him!

Ezekiel 11:19; II Corinthians 5:17; Matthew 5:8

July 5

Daily Devotion for DESTINY:

Hosea 14:9 (English Standard Version) - Whoever is wise, let him understand these things; whoever is discerning, let him know them; for the ways of the Lord are right, and the upright walk in them, but transgressors stumble in them.

It is Wisdom Day! In our scripture today, Israel is encouraged to repent and return unto God and away from their idols. The wise will profit from the message of repentance that the Prophet Hosea was bringing them.

If we are wise and able to discern (perceive; know) the times that we are living in, we would also repent and turn back to God. The ways of the Lord are right, and it is the responsibility of the righteous to walk in them.

This year, let's be wise and discerning and help our brothers and sisters who are stumbling to walk in the ways of the Lord.

Psalms 107:43; Proverbs 1:5-6; Isaiah 26:7

July 6

Daily Devotion for DESTINY:

Philippians 4:6 (English Standard Version) - **6** do not be anxious about anything, but in everything by prayer and supplication with thanksgiving let your requests be made known to God.

It is Thankful Day! In the days that we are living in, many people are acquainted with anxiety. We often feel anxious about our finances, our health and our children. The list goes on and on.

Jesus makes it clear in Matthew 6:25-34 that anxiety comes from focusing on our problems instead of the solution. What is the solution? Prayer accompanied by thanksgiving. These are the power twins!

This year, let's make prayer and thanksgiving a part of our daily lives so that we can experience peace in situations that would make others anxious!

I Peter 5:7; Psalms 55:22; I Thessalonians 5:17-18

July 7

Daily Devotion for DESTINY:

John 20:30-31 (English Standard Version) - **30** Now Jesus did many other signs in the presence of the disciples, which are not written in this book; **31** but these are written so that you may believe that Jesus is the Christ, the Son of God, and that by believing you may have life in his name.

Happy Faith Day! Our scripture today is the ending of the story of the Resurrection of Jesus and the events following. It describes the purpose of this book of the bible. There is a purpose for all of the scripture that is written.

Some scripture shows us what we should be doing and some scripture shows us what we should not be doing. The scripture goes on to say that Jesus did many more signs and wonders in the presence of the disciples that is not written in this book.

These signs and wonders were written so that we would have faith in Jesus as the Son of God. This year, as we read the scriptures, let's continue to build our faith and live the life that God has ordained for us!

I John 4:15; John 3:15-16; John 3:36

July 8

Daily Devotion for DESTINY:

I Corinthians 2:9-10 (New King James Version) -**9** But as it is written: "Eye has not seen, nor ear heard, Nor have entered into the heart of man the things which God has prepared for those who love Him."[a] **10** But God has revealed *them* to us through His Spirit. For the Spirit searches all things, yes, the deep things of God.

When the scripture says, "As it is written", this means that it is something that has already been written prior to now. In this case, the Prophet Isaiah had spoken these words in Isaiah 64:4.

There are some things about our lives which includes our purpose, our assignment and our destiny that are not evident immediately. These are the things that we must consult and seek the Holy Spirit to reveal to us.

This year, let's ask the Holy Spirit to reveal the deep things that God has planned for us to our hearts. They are only a mystery because He is waiting on us to ask Him to reveal them to us.

Isaiah 64:4; James 1:12; Romans 8:28

July 9

Daily Devotion for DESTINY:

Matthew 6:10 (Amplified Bible, classic edition) - Your kingdom come, Your will be done on earth as it is in heaven.

A short scripture today, but a very powerful one! According to Luke 17:21, every born-again believer has The Kingdom of God (aka The Kingdom of Heaven) within them. Romans 14:17 describes The Kingdom of God as righteousness, peace and joy in the Holy Ghost. Simply put, it is God's way of doing things.

Our scripture today is a verse from The Lord's Prayer. Jesus taught us to pray that God's Kingdom will come on earth as it is written in Heaven. Each one of our individual assignments play a significant role in the Kingdom of God being manifested on earth.

This year, let's follow our assignments to our destination so that God can manifest His Kingdom here on earth!

Luke 17:21; Romans 14:17; John 4:34

July 10

Daily Devotion for DESTINY:

I Timothy 4:15 (The Amplified Bible, classic edition) - **15** Practice *and* cultivate *and* meditate upon these duties; throw yourself wholly into them [as your ministry], so that your progress may be evident to everybody.

Happy Meditation Day! We are inundated with many types of meditation. I think that it is very important to make sure that we are practicing biblical meditation and not one of the many other types of meditation.

Some people confuse bible reading with biblical meditation. It is important to read the bible; however, it is equally important to mediate on the Word of God. In biblical meditation, we focus our minds on a particular subject so that what was once a concept becomes a reality in our lives.

This year, let's perfect meditating on the Word of God. You will be amazed at the insight and fresh revelation that you will receive and the direction that your life will take.

Joshua 1:8; Psalms 143:5; Psalms 119:97

July 11

Daily Devotion for DESTINY:

Colossians 3:5 (English Standard Version) - **5** Put to death therefore what is earthly in you:[a] sexual immorality, impurity, passion, evil desire, and covetousness, which is idolatry.

It is Transformation Day! Our scripture today summaries what it means to live a transformed life. It means to put to death any and everything that belongs to our earthly (fleshly) nature.

How do we crucify our flesh? The answer is found in Romans 12:2. Once we have accepted Jesus into our lives, our spirit is renewed. We must then transform our minds to think like our renewed spirit. We do this by meditating on the Word of God.

As we meditate on the Word of God, we will find ourselves feeding our flesh less often. Anything that you do not feed will eventually die. This year, let's meditate on the Word of God, crucify our flesh and live the transformed life that God intended for us!

Romans 12:2; Galatians 5:19-21; Galatians 5:24

July 12

Daily Devotion for DESTINY:

I Corinthians 2:6-7 (English Standard Version) - **6** Yet among the mature we do impart wisdom, although it is not a wisdom of this age or of the rulers of this age, who are doomed to pass away. **7** But we impart a secret and hidden wisdom of God, which God decreed before the ages for our glory.

Today is a very special day to me. It is my birthday! It is the day that I started my assignment in this earth. This has not always been the case, but today, I can honestly say that I am enjoying my journey! My prayer is that God will continue to impart His wisdom into me as I walk the path to my destiny.

In our scripture today, the apostle Paul is explaining the wisdom that God imparts to the spiritually mature. Even though Paul was a deep thinker, he always brought his knowledge down to a level so that everyone could understand what he was teaching them.

So it is with God. God's wisdom is supernatural. That is why James 1:5 tells us that if we lack wisdom, we should ask God. He will impart wisdom to us according to our level of understanding. As we grow in God, so will our wisdom.

This year, let's allow the Holy Spirit to continue to impart God's wisdom to us and become the mature Christians that God intended for us to be.

James 1:5; James 3:15; II Corinthians 4:4

July 13

Daily Devotion for DESTINY:

Psalms 106:1 (Amplified Bible, classic edition) - **1** Praise the Lord! (Hallelujah!) O give thanks to the Lord, for He is good; for His mercy *and* loving-kindness endure forever!

We made it to Thankful Day! I celebrated another year of life yesterday and I am so thankful that the Lord allowed me another year to run (not walk) towards my destiny!

Our scripture today was included in a song that the Priests and Levites sang when the Ark of the Covenant was brought into their midst. The Ark of the Covenant was a very sacred representation of the Presence of the Lord.

If you want to bring the Lord in the midst of your situation, begin to praise and worship Him. He will bring you out victoriously!

Psalms 107:1; Psalms 105:1; I Chronicles 16:34

July 14

Daily Devotion for DESTINY:

Romans 10:10 (The Amplified Bible, classic edition) - **10** For with the heart a person believes (adheres to, trusts in, and relies on Christ) and so is justified (declared righteous, acceptable to God), and with the mouth he confesses (declares openly and speaks out freely his faith) *and* confirms [his] salvation.

Happy Faith Day! Just as we had to have faith to receive the Lord into our lives, we must remain in faith to live the purposeful life that He designed for each and every one of us individually.

When we accepted the Lord into our lives, we made the declaration with our mouths. Luke 6:45 explains why this confession is necessary. It is because out of the abundance of our heart, our mouths speak.

This year, let's make it a point to speak the things that are in our faith-filled hearts and run towards our destiny with all of our might! Time is winding up!

Romans 10:9; Luke 8:15; I John 4:15

July 15

Daily Devotion for DESTINY:

Acts 20:22-24 (New International Version) - **22** "And now, compelled by the Spirit, I am going to Jerusalem, not knowing what will happen to me there. **23** I only know that in every city the Holy Spirit warns me that prison and hardships are facing me. **24** However, I consider my life worth nothing to me; my only aim is to finish the race and complete the task the Lord Jesus has given me—the task of testifying to the good news of God's grace.

Our scripture today is part of a farewell speech that Paul made to the elders of the church in Ephesus. He was on his way to Jerusalem where he was compelled by the Holy Spirit to go. Paul did not know specifically what he faced in Jerusalem, but he knew that he would be going to prison because of the gospel that he preached.

As Christians, we must adopt the same attitude that Paul had. We must run (not walk) towards our destiny! In most cases, there will definitely be hardships awaiting us there; but just like Paul, our only aim must be to complete the task that God has given us.

If we keep moving forward, in the end we will have the same testimony as Paul, "I have fought the good fight, I have finished the course, I have kept the faith, now there is stored up for me a crown of righteousness!

Acts 21:13; Acts 20:21; Acts 11:23

July 16

Daily Devotion for DESTINY:

Psalms 138:8 (English Standard Version) - The Lord will fulfill his purpose for me; your steadfast love, O Lord, endures forever. Do not forsake the work of your hands.

What is on your heart today? What are you concerned about? If it concerns you, then it concerns God. As a parent, I am concerned about whatever (it doesn't matter how big or how small) concerns my babies. I will do everything in my power to soothe their concern.

So it is with our Heavenly Father. If we allow Him, He will fulfill His purpose in our lives. He loves us so much that He will perfect (bring to maturity) those things that concerns us.

This year, let's allow God to do what He does best. BE GOD! He will not forsake the work of His hands over our lives.

Philippians 1:6; I Thessalonians 5:24; Psalms 57:2

July 17

Daily Devotion for DESTINY:

Matthew 4:4 (The Amplified Bible, classic edition) - **4** But He replied, it has been written, Man shall not live *and* be upheld *and* sustained by bread alone, but by every word that comes forth from the mouth of God.

Happy Meditation Day! Soon after Jesus was declared to be the Son of God and the Savior of the world, He was tempted by the devil. Accepting Jesus into our lives and seeking our assignment and purpose in life does not exempt us from being tempted. Quite the opposite! Once we make the decision to do the thing that we were born to do, temptation will follow!

Jesus is our example of how to handle this temptation. Even though He is the word wrapped in flesh, He still used the Word to defeat the devil. This is why we must meditate on the Word of God and hide it in our hearts. It is our weapon against the temptations that we will encounter on our way to our destiny.

This year, let's build up our arsenal of the Word of God so that we can defeat the enemy on every level!

Luke 4:4; Romans 15:4; Ephesians 6:17

July 18

Daily Devotion for DESTINY:

Ephesians 4:22-24 (English Standard Version) - **22** to put off your old self,[a] which belongs to your former manner of life and is corrupt through deceitful desires, **23** and to be renewed in the spirit of your minds, **24** and to put on the new self, created after the likeness of God in true righteousness and holiness.

It is Transformation Day! The thought of a transformed life brings most people joy; however, when we think of what we have to go through to live a transformed life, we are sometimes a little hesitant. The idea of change sounds good, but many do not want to go through the process that brings change.

The Christian life is a transformed life. Repentance in the life of a born-again believer becomes a lifestyle and not just a one-time event. Our spirit is transformed the moment that we accept the Lord into our lives, then we spend the rest of our lives becoming like God.

We should be able to see the difference between the person that we were last year and the person that we are today. Let's continue to renew our minds with the Word of God and the results will be a transformed life!

Romans 6:6; James 1:21; Ephesians 2:3

July 19

Daily Devotion for DESTINY:

Proverbs 8:35 (The Amplified Bible, classic edition) - ^{35} For whoever finds me [Wisdom] finds life and draws forth *and* obtains favor from the Lord. ^{36} But he who misses me *or* sins against me wrongs *and* injures himself; all who hate me love *and* court death.

It is Wisdom Day! The way that we treat wisdom determines the path that our lives will take. If we seek wisdom, we will obtain the favor of God. If we neglect wisdom, the scriptures say that we love death. Simply put, wisdom brings life to our soul (mind, will, emotions) and the lack of wisdom brings death.

In case you are still unclear on the meaning of wisdom, it is knowing the perfect will of an Infinite God about each and every aspect of our lives. Wisdom must be sought diligently. We begin by asking God for wisdom, but we seek it by meditating on the Word of God where much of His wisdom is found.

If you make an effort to seek the wisdom of God, you will find it and obtain the favor of the Lord!

Proverbs 3:13-18; Proverbs 12:2; Colossians 3:3

July 20

Daily Devotion for DESTINY:

Psalms 9:1 (The Amplified Bible, classic edition) - **1** I will praise You, O Lord, with my whole heart; I will show forth (recount and tell aloud) all Your marvelous works *and* wonderful deeds!

It is Thankful Day! God understands that thanksgiving is not usually the first reaction that we have when we face trials and tribulations. There is great value in choosing to be thankful even when the emotions are not there.

Hebrews 13:15 encourages us to sacrifice a praise unto God. There are sometimes when God does not come through as we thought He would. Maybe the doctor's report came back positive. Maybe our home goes into foreclosure. Maybe God just seems very far away. To be able to praise God during those times require sacrifice.

This year, let's be determined to not only praise God when things are going as planned, but to praise him even harder when things are going the opposite of our plan. Remind yourself that no matter the circumstances, God is still good and worthy to be praised!

Isaiah 12:1;I Chronicles 16:24; Psalms 51:15

July 21

Daily Devotion for DESTINY:

Galatians 3:11 (The Amplified Bible, classic edition) - **11** Now it is evident that no person is justified (declared righteous and brought into right standing with God) through the Law, for the Scripture says, The man in right standing with God [the just, the righteous] shall live by *and* out of faith *and* he who through *and* by faith is declared righteous *and* in right standing with God shall live.

Happy Faith Day! We must make the Word of God the authority in our lives. We are made righteous by our belief in God's word. Galatians 3:6 tells us that Abraham believed God and it was accounted unto him for righteousness. The scriptures also tell us that the just shall live by faith.

As Christians, we should obey the law; however, the law cannot justify us in the eyes of God or bring blessings into our lives. Faith in God attracts blessings to us.

This year, let's not only believe what God says, but let's act on it. Acting on the Word of God produces results. As the saying goes, Action speaks louder than words!

Habakkuk 2:4; Galatians 3:6; Romans 1:17

July 22

Daily Devotion for DESTINY:

John 17:4 (The Amplified Bible, classic edition) - **4** I have glorified You down here on the earth by completing the work that You gave Me to do.

Jesus glorified the father by completing the work that He had given him to do. What this means is that we glorify God when we complete our destiny. I want to talk to the Christians that are satisfied with just going to heaven. Even though that is better than the alternative, I want to encourage you to not be satisfied with anything short of completing your destiny.

To those who are on the path to your destiny, I want to encourage you to continue on that path. We demonstrate God's power here on earth when we passionately pursue our assignment.

This year, let's honor God through our obedience to His commands for our lives. In the end, we will have the testimony that we have glorified God by completing the work that He has given us to do!

Acts 20:24; Luke 22:37; II Timothy 4:7

July 23

Daily Devotion for DESTINY:

II Timothy 3:16 (The Amplified bible, classic edition) - **16** Every Scripture is God-breathed (given by His inspiration) and profitable for instruction, for reproof *and* conviction of sin, for correction of error *and* discipline in obedience, [and] for training in righteousness (in holy living, in conformity to God's will in thought, purpose, and action),

I was glad when they said unto me, Let us go into the House of the Lord! There is much controversy about the validity of the bible. Please understand that I am one who believes that the bible is God-breathed and that every word was written for a purpose.

Our scripture today tells us the purpose of EVERY scripture in the bible. Some scripture is given for instruction, some for conviction of sin, some to correct the errors in our lives as we learn obedience and some to train us how to live holy before a Holy God. In other words, the scripture teaches us what to do as well as what NOT to do as we pursue our destiny.

Keep this in mind as you head to church this morning to hear the preached Word of God. If you apply it to your life in its proper perspective, you will never be the same!

Romans 15:4; Hebrews 4:12; Mark 12:24

July 24

Daily Devotion for DESTINY:

John 8:31-32 (New King James Version) - **1** Then Jesus said to those Jews who believed Him, "If you abide in My word, you are My disciples indeed. **32** And you shall know the truth, and the truth shall make you free."

Happy Meditation Day! Jesus gives us the true meaning of discipleship in our scripture today. He said that if we abide (meditate on); remain) in His word, we are His disciples.

It is very important that we abide in God's word. It is the truth of God's word that makes us free from the bondages that life offers us each and every day.

This year, let's bring our focus and attention to the Word of God and become true disciples for Christ. As we gain our freedom through the Word of God, we can begin to free our brothers and sisters!

Romans 8:2; John 17:17; Psalms 25:5

July 25

Daily Devotion for DESTINY:

I Corinthians 2:16 (The Amplified Bible, classic edition) - **16** For who has known *or* understood the mind (the counsels and purposes) of the Lord so as to guide *and* instruct Him *and* give Him knowledge? But we have the mind of Christ (the Messiah) *and* do hold the thoughts (feelings and purposes) of His heart.

It is Transformation Day! The ultimate goal of renewing our minds is so that we will have the mind of Christ. A renewed mind will cause our lives to be transformed into a life that is pleasing to God.

This quote by Mahatma Gandhi helps us to realize the importance of a renewed mind: Your beliefs become your thoughts, your thoughts become your words, your words become your actions, your actions become your habits, your habits become your values, your values become your destiny."

To sum it up, our destiny begins in our minds!

John 15:15; Jeremiah 23:18; Romans 11:34

July 26

Daily Devotion for DESTINY:

Ephesians 5:15-17 (English Standard Version) - **15** Look carefully then how you walk, not as unwise but as wise,**16** making the best use of the time, because the days are evil.**17** Therefore do not be foolish but understand what the will of the Lord is.

It is Wisdom Day! God has allotted each one of us a certain length of time to fulfill our destiny. Our scripture today tells us to walk wisely by making the most of the time that we have been allotted.

God is a God of purpose and we must be in line with His purpose. Jesus prepared Himself 30 years for a 3 1/2-year ministry. He lived to accomplish the purpose of the Father and so do we!

Time is a very precious commodity. While all of our times is in God's hands, He wants us to be wise and redeem the time that He has given us to fulfill our purpose. If we want our lives to count in eternity, we must be wise about how we spend our time on earth because those decisions will follow us into eternity.

Colossians 4:5; Amos 5:13; Romans 12:2

July 27

Daily Devotion for DESTINY:

Psalms 116:12 (The Amplified Bible, classic edition) - **12** What shall I render to the Lord for all His benefits toward me? [How can I repay Him for all His bountiful dealings?]

It is Thankful Day! Our scripture today is a Thanksgiving Psalms. It is not clear whether David wrote it in recognition of any particular occasion, or whether he was just thinking on the many deliverances that God had brought him through.

Whatever the occasion, David had learned the secret to pleasing God to the point that God said that David was a man after God's own heart (I Samuel 13:14). In addition to having a repentant heart (which is very important), David also had a very thankful heart.

Let us make it a point this year to repent swiftly and develop a thankful heart. Romans 2:4 tells us that the goodness of God leads to repentance. God has been good to us, now it is time for us to repent and be thankful!

Psalms 103:2; II Corinthians 5:14-15; Romans 12:1

July 28

Daily Devotion for DESTINY:

Hebrews 11:1 (The Amplified Bible, classic edition) - Now faith is the assurance (the confirmation, [a]the title deed) of the things [we] hope for, being the proof of things [we] do not see *and* the conviction of their reality [faith perceiving as real fact what is not revealed to the senses].

Happy Faith Day! Today we are going back to the basics. Our scripture is the definition of the faith that we as Christians are striving to attain, Faith is having the assurance (conviction) that God is going to do just what He said that He will do.

The word conviction is used in court when trying a crime. A conviction comes about when irrefutable facts convinces a judge or a jury of guilt. A conviction is made because the evidence has been provided.

This year, let's allow the irrefutable facts and the evidence that God has already provided in each of our lives to assure (convict) us that the things that God said shall surely come to pass even though we cannot yet see them!

II Corinthians 5:7;II Corinthians 4:18;Hebrews 11:27

July 29

Daily Devotion for DESTINY:

Ephesians 2:10 (The Amplified Bible, classic edition) - **10** For we are God's [own] handiwork (His workmanship), [a]recreated in Christ Jesus, [born anew] that we may do those good works which God predestined (planned beforehand) for us [taking paths which He prepared ahead of time], that we should walk in them [living the good life which He prearranged and made ready for us to live].

Each and every one of us was uniquely created by God. We are His workmanship. We are His handiwork. Psalms 139:14 tells us that we are fearfully and wonderfully made. I just want to speak to your self-esteem today. God made you perfect for your purpose!

He took the time to not only uniquely create us, but to give each one of us our own unique purpose. As if that was not enough, He went before us and created the path that we should take to get to our destiny! Are you praising Him yet?

My path may not be your path and vice versa, but every path leads to one destination….The Perfect Will of God! If you are not already on the path to your destiny, I encourage you to allow God to place you there. Enjoy your journey!

Psalms 139:14; Philippians 2:13; Colossians 1:10

July 30

Daily Devotion for DESTINY:

John 10:10 (The Amplified Bible, classic edition) - **10** The thief comes only in order to steal and kill and destroy. I came that they may have *and* enjoy life, and have it in abundance (to the full, till it [a] overflows).

It is very important that we not only know our purpose, but we should know our enemy's purpose and Jesus' purpose if we are going to make it to our destination. To keep satan from getting the advantage over us, God will not allow us to be ignorant of the devil's devices that he tries to use to stop us from fulfilling our destiny (II Corinthians 2:11).

The devil comes to steal, kill and destroy. If you are experiencing situations that can kill you, steal from you and/or destroy you, then you know that it came from satan and that you have power over both him and the situation.

This year, let's allow God to fulfill His purpose in our lives. He desires that we enjoy abundant life on our way to our destiny!

Luke 19:10; II Corinthians 2:11; John 3:17

July 31

Daily Devotion for DESTINY:

Ii Peter 2:9 (The Amplified Bible, classic edition) - **9** Now if [all these things are true, then be sure] the Lord knows how to rescue the Godly out of temptations *and* trials, and how to keep the unGodly under chastisement until the day of judgment *and* doom,

Happy Meditation Day! Now that we have the basic understanding of what meditation is, we are going to meditate on God's faithfulness. We should not only meditate on today's scripture, but we should keep it tucked away in our hearts.

God knows how to rescue us out of temptations and trials. He always makes a way of escape (I Corinthians 10:13). God also knows how to keep the unrighteous under chastisement until He judges them. What this means is that vengeance belongs to God and He will repay (Romans 12:19).

This year, let's meditate on God's faithfulness to us and what He has called us to do and leave everything else to Him. He is more than able to handle that which we commit into His hands!

I Corinthians 10:13; Romans 12:19; Revelation 3:10

August

Being confident of this, that he who began a good work in you will carry it on to completion until the day of Christ Jesus.

Philippians 1:6 (NIV)

August 1

Daily Devotion for DESTINY:

Philippians 1:6 (The Amplified Bible, classic edition) - **6** And I am convinced *and* sure of this very thing, that He Who began a good work in you will continue until the day of Jesus Christ [right up to the time of His return], developing [that good work] *and* perfecting *and* bringing it to full completion in you.

It is Transformation Day! Over the past few weeks, we have been learning what it means to be transformed by renewing our minds. To sum it up, transformation means a renewal from a thought life that no longer conforms to the ways of the world to a thought life that pleases God.

A renewed mind will manifest itself in our actions. The bible teaches us that a transformed life causes us to bear fruit in every good work and grow in the knowledge of God (Colossians 1:10). Evidence of our transformation is seen in the way we continue to reflect the likeness of our father.

As we press towards our journey of transformation, will the world be able to look at us and say, He (God) IS the Father!", or will they say He (God) IS NOT the father?"

Philippians 2:13; Ephesians 4:12; Psalms 138:8

August 2

Daily Devotion for DESTINY:

Proverbs 26:12 (New International Version) - Whoever is wise, let him attend to these things; let them consider the steadfast love of the Lord.

It is Wisdom Day! A truly wise person will understand that God is a merciful God and that His desire is that all thing work together for our good.

What things will wise men attend to (observe) according to our scripture? At some point or time in all of our lives, we all have experienced the Loving-kindness of the Lord. A wise man will keep these experiences tucked away in his/ her heart.

This year, let's observe the attributes of a Loving God and pattern our lives after the example that Jesus set for us. When we do this, we will perceive that God is worthy of our confidence and will be on the path to become that wise man / woman that God desires for us to be!

Hosea 14:9; Jeremiah 9:12; Ephesians 1:15

August 3

Daily Devotion for DESTINY:

Psalms 103:2 (The Amplified Bible, classic edition) - **2** Bless (affectionately, gratefully praise) the Lord, O my soul, and forget not [one of] all His benefits

Welcome to Thankful Day! In our scripture today, David is having his own personal devotion. He is setting his soul (mind, will & emotions) up to praise the Lord. To bless the Lord means to say good things about Him in the spirit of gratitude and admiration.

Our trials and tribulations can blind us to the fact that God is continually at work in our lives. During these times, we must do as David did and command our souls to praise the Lord. We do this by fixing our eyes on the acts, provisions and deliverances that the Lord has done for us in the past. If He did it then, He will do it again!

This year, let's hold fast to the truths that we know about God. When you meditate on these truths, the end result will be praise to a Loving God!

Psalms 105:5; Isaiah 63:7; Psalms 116:12

August 4

Daily Devotion for DESTINY:

John 4:42 (The Amplified Bible, classic edition) - **42** And they told the woman, Now we no longer believe (trust, have faith) just because of what you said; for we have heard Him ourselves [personally], and we know that He truly is the Savior of the world, *the Christ.*

Happy Faith Day! Our scripture today is the result of a conversation that Jesus had with the woman at the well. While Jesus was on His way from Judea to Galilee, He felt in His Spirit that he should go through Samaria. While in Samaria, He ministered to a woman at the well. Jesus went to Samaria to set this one woman free!

After Jesus ministered to the Samaritan woman, she believed what she had heard and knew that Jesus was the Messiah. She could not wait to not only share her faith, but to bring others with her to meet the man that was able to tell her all about her prior sins AND set her free!

Have you had an encounter with Jesus that stirred up your faith? Share your experiences with your friends and neighbors. Stir up their faith and lead them to Jesus! Our goal this year is "Each one, Reach one"!

I John 4:14; John 1:29; Acts 4:12

August 5

Daily Devotion for DESTINY:

Psalms 37:1-2 (The Amplified Bible, classic edition) - **1** Fret not yourself because of evildoers, neither be envious against those who work unrighteousness (that which is not upright or in right standing with God). **2** For they shall soon be cut down like the grass, and wither as the green herb.

Does it feel to you that sometimes the most evil, hateful people are the ones that seemingly have the most success in life? Things are not always as they seem. Our scripture today lets us know that their success in life is temporary.

It is very easy to become envious of evildoers' success and begin to fret. Do not be tempted to give in to these feelings. The scripture goes on to tell us the benefit of trusting and obeying God even (and especially) when it doesn't seem like the most successful thing to do.

This year, let's commit our way to the Lord where we will find favor and success with both God and man! (Proverbs 3:4).

Proverbs 23:27; Proverbs 3:31; Proverbs 24:1

August 6

Daily Devotion for DESTINY:

Psalms 37:4 (The Amplified Bible, classic edition) - **4** Delight yourself also in the Lord, and He will give you the desires *and* secret petitions of your heart.

How do you know what God created you to do; your specific assignment on earth? Our scripture today gives us insight into just one of the ways that we can discover our assignment. As the year goes on, everyone who desires will learn not only how to discover your assignment, but also how to fulfill your assignment.

When we delight ourselves in the Lord, we will find that our carnal desires begin to drop off and our desires begin to line up with God's desire for us. Pay attention to your Godly desires. It is God who placed them in your heart to accomplish your assignment here on this earth.

This year, let's make sure that the desires of our hearts are the desires that God placed there. If they are, God will move heaven and earth to make sure that you receive the desires of your heart!

John 15:7; Psalms 145:19; John 15:16

August 7

Daily Devotion for DESTINY:

Psalms 1:1-2 (New International Version) -
Blessed is the one
who does not walk in step with the wicked
or stand in the way that sinners take
or sit in the company of mockers,
²but whose delight is in the law of the LORD,
and who meditates on his Law Day and night.

It is Meditation Day! Yesterday, we learned that one way to discover our assignment is to delight ourselves in the Lord. This will cause our carnal desires to become Godly desires. This week, I am going to share some of the ways that we can delight ourselves in the Lord.

Our scripture today tells us that a blessed man/woman's delight is in the law of the Lord. He/She meditates on God's law (His word) day and night. God's word sanctifies our thinking bringing our desires into submission to God's desires for us.

This year, let's delight ourselves in the Lord by meditating on God's word, applying it to our lives and watching our carnal desires change to Godly desires!

Joshua 1:8; Psalms 119:35; Romans 7:22

August 8

Daily Devotion for DESTINY:

Colossians 3:2 (The Amplified Bible, classic edition) - **2** And set your minds *and* keep them set on what is above (the higher things), not on the things that are on the earth.

It is Transformation Day! We are going to continue to learn how to delight ourselves in the Lord. Another way to delight yourself in the Lord is to set you mind on eternal things. If we are going to win the spiritual war, we must focus on things above.

God wants us to love things above. He wants us to delight in the things that He has planned for us. It must start with a choice on our part. We must choose to transform our minds so that they are set on things above and not on the temporary things on earth.

This year, let's take the first step by asking God to make His desires for us our desires!

Matthew 16:23; I Chronicles 22:19; Matthew 6:19

August 9

Daily Devotion for DESTINY:

II Kings 17:38-39 (New International Version) - **38** Do not forget the covenant I have made with you, and do not worship other Gods. **39** Rather, worship the Lord your God; it is he who will deliver you from the hand of all your enemies."

Normally, today would be Wisdom Day, but worship is so heavy on my heart, that I would like to make it Worship Day. Worship is my favorite tool that I use to delight myself in the Lord. We must remember that we do not worship God for His blessings. We worship God just because He is God.

Anyone can (and should) praise God. Psalms 150:6 (The Amplified Bible, classic edition) says,

⁶Let everything that has breath *and* every breath of life praise the Lord! Praise the Lord! (Hallelujah!) Everyone that has breath should praise the Lord for everything that He does for us. Worship; however, is reserved for those who have a personal relationship with God.

This year, let's delight ourselves in the Lord by elevating our praise into worship!

Luke 1:71; Matthew 10:28; Luke 1:74-75

August 10

Daily Devotion for DESTINY:

Psalms 107:8 (English Standard Version) - Let them thank the Lord for his steadfast love, for his wondrous works to the children of man!

It is Thankful Day! We are delighting ourselves in the Lord today by letting Him know how thankful we are for His unfailing love and for His marvelous acts.

Our praises to the Lord must be personal. With all of the negativity in the world today, it is crucial that we, as Christians, share the reason why we are thankful in spite of what is going on around us.

This year, let's resolve and purpose in our hearts that we will be thankful in whatever state we are in because there is always someone somewhere in worst shape than we are!

Isaiah 63:7; Psalms 147:1; Psalms 111:4

August 11

Daily Devotion for DESTINY:

I John 5:4 (New Living Translation) - **4** For every child of God defeats this evil world, and we achieve this victory through our faith.

Happy Faith Day! Today, let's delight ourselves in the Lord by walking by faith and not by sight. God delights in His children when we gain victory over the tests and trials that we face. We gain victory through our faith.

How do we attain the faith that brings us victory in all our circumstances? We must hear the word of God, not only with our ears but with our heart. Victorious faith is knowing in your heart of hearts that greater is He that is within you than he that is in the world.

This year, let's not focus on the storms that we will encounter in this life, but let us focus on the victories that we will experience because we trust God!

I Corinthians 15:57; I John 4:4; John 16:33

August 12

Daily Devotion for DESTINY:

Hebrews 5:12-13 (Living Bible Translation) - **12-13** You have been Christians a long time now, and you ought to be teaching others, but instead you have dropped back to the place where you need someone to teach you all over again the very first principles in God's Word. You are like babies who can drink only milk, not old enough for solid food. And when a person is still living on milk it shows he isn't very far along in the Christian life and doesn't know much about the difference between right and wrong. He is still a baby Christian!

I want to address something that is heavy on my heart this morning. It is the importance of continuing to grow in the things of God. Many of our older saints have come to the point where they feel like they have been a Christian so long that they have "seen and heard it all"! The truth about Christianity is that if you are not growing, you are going backwards. There is no standing still in this faith.

I want to encourage the young and old alike to do everything that you can to continue to grow in God. You are welcome to join me every morning as I meditate on the word of God, transform my mind, worship the Father, Praise Him for His mighty acts and build my faith through my Daily Devotions that will lead you to your destiny!

I Peter 2:2; Hebrews 6:1; Titus 2:3-4

August 13

Daily Devotion for DESTINY:

Ephesians 4:11-12 (King James Version) - **11** And he gave some, apostles; and some, prophets; and some, evangelists; and some, pastors and teachers; **12** For the perfecting of the saints, for the work of the ministry, for the edifying of the body of Christ:

I would like to continue where I left off yesterday; the importance of continual growth in God. Another way that we grow spiritually is to assemble ourselves with other believers (Hebrews 10:25).

I want to stress that God is a God of purpose. Our scripture today tells us the purpose of our local churches. God put ministry gifts (Apostles, Prophets, Evangelists, Pastors & Teachers) in our local churches to mature (grow us up) in the things of God.

This year, let's commit to a bible-believing church that will help us grow in our knowledge of God. As we learn more about God, we will learn more about ourselves and His plans for us!

Jeremiah 3:15; Ephesians 3:5; Acts 20:28

August 14

Daily Devotion for DESTINY:

Psalms 104:34 (The Amplified Bible, classic edition) - **34** May my meditation be sweet to Him; as for me, I will rejoice in the Lord.

Happy Meditation Day! The bible puts a high value on meditation. Biblical meditation includes purposely thinking and pondering on God's word. Medication gives us inner and moral strength that manifests in our behavior.

Meditation transfers the Word of God from our minds to our spirits. In our minds, we can still reason out the Word of God; however, in our spirits, it does not need an explanation. We just know that it is true.

This year, let's consistently meditate on the Word of God. When we do, we will begin to think, talk and act like God. We will become a reflection of His word!

Psalms 1:2; Psalms 119:15-16; Psalms 32:11

August 15

Daily Devotion for DESTINY:

I John 1:9 (English Standard Version) - **9** If we confess our sins, he is faithful and just to forgive us our sins and to cleanse us from all unrighteousness.

It is Transformation Day! The ultimate transformation begins with confessing our sins to God. He is the one against whom the sin was committed, and He is the one who can forgive us of sin. We can only truly confess our sins because the Holy Spirit has convicted us and filled us with Godly sorrow.

Transformation comes when we receive the forgiveness that God offers us once we repent. When God cleanses us from sin, He also removes the guilt of the sin so that we don't have to continue to feel condemned.

If you have not already done so, confess your sins to God and allow Him to cleanse you of all unrighteousness; then begin to live the transformed life that God desires for each one of us!

Psalms 32:5; Proverbs 28:13; I Corinthians 6:11

August 16

Daily Devotion for DESTINY:

Proverbs 18:15 (The Amplified Bible, classic edition) - **15** The mind of the prudent is ever getting knowledge, and the ear of the wise is ever seeking (inquiring for and craving) knowledge.

It's Wisdom Day! Intelligent people are always ready to learn. Their ears are always open to knowledge. The man / woman that is truly desirous of wisdom grasps on to useful information and apply it to their lives.

We must make it a point to associate with wise men and women so that we may attain more wisdom and knowledge. Bishop T. D. Jakes often say that if you are the smartest (wisest) person in your circle, then your circle is too small.

This year, let's expand our circle to include wise men and women that will make positive deposits into our lives. Let us also share the wisdom that we have gained over the years with those coming behind us.

Proverbs 23:23; Proverbs 10:14; Proverbs 9:9

August 17

Daily Devotion for DESTINY:

I Chronicles 16:8 (English Standard Version) - Oh give thanks to the Lord; call upon his name; make known his deeds among the peoples!

On this Thankful Day, we must make sure that we glorify God both alone and in the presence of others. When we recognize and affirm God's goodness through our praise, we show others the loving character and nature of our God.

Praise benefits us because it takes our minds off our problems and bring our focus back to God's power, mercy and love. One of the key things that sets the Christian apart from the world is our thankful spirit.

This year, let's focus on our mission to reach others by telling them about God's goodness and by being an example of the transformation that comes with living a thankful life.

Isaiah 12:4; I Corinthians 1:2; I Chronicles 16:34

August 18

Daily Devotion for DESTINY:

Luke 17:6 (English Standard Version) - **6** And the Lord said, "If you had faith like a grain of mustard seed, you could say to this mulberry tree, 'Be uprooted and planted in the sea,' and it would obey you.

Happy Faith Day! Our scripture today is the result of Jesus teaching the disciples how to forgive. Faith and forgiveness go hand in hand. We, as Christians, are required to forgive offenses from our brothers and sisters.

The disciples realized that it takes faith to forgive an offense and walk in love especially when you are offended by the same person constantly. They asked the Lord to increase their faith so that they can continue to forgive.

Jesus responded by letting them know that we can accomplish the impossible even with small faith; however, His desire is that our faith continues to grow into great faith!

Matthew 17:20; Mark 9:23; Matthew 21:21

August 19

Daily Devotion for DESTINY:

II Kings 2:13-14 (English Standard Version) - **13** And he took up the cloak of Elijah that had fallen from him and went back and stood on the bank of the Jordan. **14** Then he took the cloak of Elijah that had fallen from him and struck the water, saying, "Where is the Lord, the God of Elijah?" And when he had struck the water, the water was parted to the one side and to the other, and Elisha went over.

Over the past few weeks, I have personally experienced several friends and family transition from their earthly home to their eternal home. It is important to note that when someone transitions from earth to glory, they do not take their mantles (an important role or responsibility that passes from one person to another) with them. These mantles are not needed in heaven.

Let us take inventory now of our divine connections to make sure that once they transition, we will be able to pick up their mantle that has been assigned to us and move forward just as Elisha did with Elijah's mantle.

This year, let us purpose in our hearts that we will not let the mantles of our friends and family lay dormant once they transition. After all, God gave them to us to part the waters for us in this life!

John 14:12; Mark 16:20; Joshua 1:1-9

August 20

Daily Devotion for DESTINY:

II Corinthians 10:5 (English Standard Version) - **5** We destroy arguments and every lofty opinion raised against the knowledge of God, and take every thought captive to obey Christ,

God wants us to progress in our purpose because that is the very reason that we were created and that is what brings Him glory. The devil tries to hinder our progress in God by playing mind games with us.

We must be careful of the memories that come to our minds to distract us. The greatest hindrance to our breakthrough is our memory. Our thoughts fuel our feelings and our feelings fuel our actions.

This year, let's destroy every thought that exalts itself against the knowledge of God and beat the devil at his own game! We can win this battle in our minds!

Hebrews 4:12; Romans 7:23; Isaiah 55:7

August 21

Daily Devotion for DESTINY:

II Timothy 2:7 (New International Version) - **7** Reflect on what I am saying, for the Lord will give you insight into all this.

Happy Meditation Day! We, in and of ourselves, do not understand the scriptures. This is why it is important that we meditate on them. When we meditate on the scriptures, it allows the Holy Spirit to reveal the meaning to us and how we should apply them to our individual lives.

As our trials increase, our understanding and application of the Word of God must increase as well! If we do our part by meditating on and applying God's word to our lives; God will do His part by bringing us out of our trials victoriously!

This year, let's make meditating on God's word part of our daily lifestyle. It is a practice that will always yield good fruit!

Joshua 1:8; Psalms 1:1; I John 5:20

August 22

Daily Devotion for DESTINY:

I John 2:3-4 (The Amplified Bible, classic edition) - **3** And this is how we may discern [[a]daily, by experience] that we are coming to know Him [to perceive, recognize, understand, and become better acquainted with Him]: if we keep (bear in mind, observe, practice) His teachings (precepts, commandments)> **4** Whoever says, I know Him [I perceive, recognize, understand, and am acquainted with Him] but fails to keep *and* obey His commandments (teachings) is a liar, and the Truth [[b]of the Gospel] is not in him.

It is Transformation Day! When we are truly transformed, we understand that God is worthy of our total obedience. The way that we can discern that we are being transformed is when we strive to live our lives according to what God says is right and not according to what society tells us is right.

The scripture goes on to say that whoever say that they know God but fail to obey His word is deceived (a liar) in the worst way. When we love someone, we try to transform ourselves into the person that pleases the person that we love.

This year, let's transform ourselves into the person that pleases God by obeying His word!

John 14:15; I John 5:3; Luke 6:46

August 23

Daily Devotion for DESTINY:

Proverbs 16:16 (The Amplified Bible, classic edition) - **16** How much better it is to get skillful *and* Godly Wisdom than gold! And to get understanding is to be chosen rather than silver.

It is Wisdom Day! Why should we desire wisdom above silver and gold? Wisdom imparts to us the power to choose the things in life that will bring us happiness. We understand that we need silver and gold (money) to function in this life; however, a wise man realizes that you can have money and not have wisdom, but you cannot have wisdom and not acquire money.

Dr. W.H. Dallinger said that the biggest hindrance to us getting wisdom is our habits. He went on to say that no influence is more powerful in our destiny than the formation of habits.

This year, let's form new habits by meditating on God's word, transforming our lives, seeking God's wisdom, being thankful and walking by faith and not by sight!

Proverbs 8:19; Luke 12:21; Matthew 16:26

August 24

Daily Devotion for DESTINY:

Psalms 30:1 (New International Version) - I will exalt you, Lord, for you lifted me out of the depths and did not let my enemies gloat over me.

It is Thankful Day! David wrote this Psalm in response to all of the deliverances that God had brought him through. We, too should advance the Kingdom of God by making known the great deeds that He has done (and is doing) for us.

God did not allow David's enemies to rejoice in his affliction. God will also not allow our enemies to rejoice as we go through our trials and tribulations as long as we praise our way through!

This year, let's advance the Kingdom of God by stepping up our praise in gratitude for all of the things that he has done and continue to do for us!

Psalms 25:2; Psalms 140;8; Psalms 41:11

August 25

Daily Devotion for DESTINY:

James 1:2-4 (The Message Bible) - **2-4** Consider it a sheer gift, friends, when tests and challenges come at you from all sides. You know that under pressure, your faith-life is forced into the open and shows its true colors. So don't try to get out of anything prematurely. Let it do its work so you become mature and well-developed, not deficient in any way.

Happy Faith Day! As we are developing our faith and learning how to walk by faith, we must understand that our faith will be tested. The purpose of our faith being tried is to bring us to maturity in our walk with God.

It doesn't matter what we say about living a life of faith. What we really believe will become evident to everyone (including ourselves) once our faith is tested. We know that we are maturing when we are able to count our trials and tribulations as joy because that is rarely our first response.

This year, let's commit ourselves to the process that makes us like Christ (spiritually mature) so that we can reap the benefits.

James 1:12: II Peter 2:9; Colossians 1:24

August 26

Daily Devotion for DESTINY:

I Corinthians 6:19-20 (English Standard Version) - **19** Or do you not know that your body is a temple of the Holy Spirit within you, whom you have from God? You are not your own, **20** for you were bought with a price. So, glorify God in your body.

We, as Christians must not only glorify God with our mouths, but we must glorify God in our bodies. It is the temple where the Holy Spirit dwells. When Jesus died on the cross and rose again, it was not only to redeem our souls, but it was to redeem our bodies as well.

Paul wrote this letter to the Corinthian church because some among the Corinthians had gotten the idea that they could do whatever they pleased as long as they "believed that there is a God". Sound familiar?

This year, let's honor God in our bodies and allow them to be an instrument of the righteousness of God.

II Corinthians 6:16; II Corinthians 5:15; Psalms 100:3

August 27

Daily Devotion for DESTINY:

Numbers 23:19 (English Standard Version) - God is not man, that he should lie, or a son of man, that he should change his mind. Has he said, and will he not do it? Or has he spoken, and will he not fulfill it?

I just want to remind everyone this morning that God cannot lie! If He said it, that thing will surely come to pass! Why? Because He speaks those things that be not as though they were, then they become!

Has God made a promise to you? Be encouraged this morning that as long as you walk in faith for the thing that He has promised, you will see it manifest. Do not be moved by what you see or feel. Focus on the promise!

This year, let's agree with everything that God has said about us and watch it come to pass in our lives!

Hebrews 6:18; I Samuel 15:29; Romans 11:29

August 28

Daily Devotion for DESTINY:

Psalms 119:48 (English Standard Version) -I will lift up my hands toward your commandments, which I love, and I will meditate on your statutes.

It is Meditation Day! Although it is a necessity to meditate, we must be very careful to make sure that our focus is on the word of God. Meditation opens our minds and makes us vulnerable to satanic attacks.

Biblical meditation detaches us from the controlling influences of the world and attaches us to the mind of Christ. It involves reflecting on biblical truth and allowing God to speak to our minds and our spirits through His word.

This year, let's internalize and personalize the scriptures so that it can affect how we think which will affect our actions.

Psalms 119:127; Psalms 1:2; Psalms 119:97

August 29

Daily Devotion for DESTINY:

II Corinthians 5:17 (The Amplified Bible, classic edition) - **17** Therefore if any person is [engrafted] in Christ (the Messiah) he is a new creation (a new creature altogether); the old [previous moral and spiritual condition] has passed away. Behold, the fresh *and* new has come!

It is Transformation Day! We now understand the importance of transforming our minds. It is much bigger than that. We must begin living in the "new" once we have made Jesus the Lord and Savior of our lives.

We should listen to messages that provoke us to think the "new" thing that God is doing in our lives. We should hang around people that challenge us to fill our minds with the word of God and hold us accountable to our new way of thinking.

This year, let's abandon our old, erroneous thoughts and allow God to break the limitations off our minds. God is doing a new thing and He wants to do it for and through us!

Ezekiel 36:26; Ephesians 4:22-24; Psalms 51:10

August 30

Daily Devotion for DESTINY:

Proverbs 14:1 (New International Version) - The wise woman builds her house but with her own hands the foolish one tears hers down.

It is Wisdom Day! I want to speak to the women today. Our scripture today tells us that a wise woman builds her house. We have heard it said that if you give a (wise) woman a house, she will give you a home; if you give her food, she will give you a meal; if you give her a seed, she will give you a baby.

On the other hand, a foolish woman will destroy her own home through idleness, laziness and negligence. This type of woman will certainly ruin her family. Whether you are single or married, seek to be the (wise) woman that builds her house.

This year, women, let's build our house on the Rock (JESUS) and allow Him to make us the virtuous (wise) women that He intended for us to be.

Proverbs 24:3-4; Ruth 4:11; Proverbs 21:9

August 31

Daily Devotion for DESTINY:

Psalms 116:12 (The Amplified Bible, classic edition) – ¹² What shall I render to the Lord for all His benefits toward me? [How can I repay Him for all His bountiful dealings? It is Thankful Day! We know that the very essence of God is love! Love gives because it delights in giving. And so it is with God. He gives with the intent of blessing us with no ulterior motive.

What can we offer God for His pure, perfect love towards us? We can offer Him a heart of Thanksgiving! We can never repay God for His goodness towards us, but we can express our gratitude by being thankful.

This year, let's receive God's love first by offering our hearts to Him, then by giving Him the ultimate return on His investment in us... Thanksgiving!

I Corinthians 6:20; Romans 12:1; Psalms 103:2

September

¹⁰For we are God's handiwork, created in Christ Jesus to do good works which God prepared in advance for us to do.

Ephesians 2:10 (NIV)

September 1

Daily Devotion for DESTINY:

I Corinthians 16:13 -(The Amplified Bible, classic edition) - **13** Be alert *and* on your guard; stand firm in your faith ([a]your conviction respecting man's relationship to God and divine things, keeping the trust and holy fervor born of faith and a part of it). Act like men *and* be courageous; grow in strength!

Happy Faith Day! In our scripture today, Paul was giving some exhortations to the Church at Corinth which is very sound advice even for us today. With everything that is going on in the world, we must stand strong in our faith if we are going to survive.

Paul's advice was addressing all of the turmoil that was going on in the church at that time, but it has a much broader application than that. It is the sum of our charge as Christians as we walk towards our destiny.

This year, let's act like men (and women) of God and stand fast in the faith. We must hold on to and defend the truths of the gospel looking unto Jesus, the author and finisher of our faith!

Joshua 1:9; Ephesians 6:10; I Corinthians 15:58

September 2

Daily Devotion for DESTINY:

Isaiah 43:18-19 (English Standard Version) - "Remember not the former things, nor consider the things of old. **19** Behold, I am doing a new thing; now it springs forth, do you not perceive it?

I will make a way in the wilderness and rivers in the desert.

Isaiah wrote this word of prophecy to the Israelites at a very trying time in their lives. They had lost everything they had and they were beginning to doubt the blessings and the land flowing with milk and honey that God had promised them.

Are you going through a trying time? Are you struggling to hang on to the word that God spoke to you? God wants to do a new thing in our lives. We must forget the former things (good and bad) from our past and allow God to do the new thing that He desires to do.

This year, let's not expect God to move for us like He has in the past. Let's keep our ears on His chest and open to His voice so that we can discern His movement and go with the flow!

II Corinthians 5:17; Revelation 21:5; Isaiah 41:18

September 3

Daily Devotion for DESTINY:

Proverbs 3:5-6 (English Standard Version) -Trust in the Lord with all your heart, and do not lean on your own understanding. **6** In all your ways acknowledge him, and he will make straight your paths.

When the bible tells us not to lean to our own understanding, it is not telling us not to think or get an understanding. It is telling us not to depend on our "own" understanding meaning conclusions that are based solely on our own perceptions.

Many times, our own understanding is not based on reality. Why trust our limited understanding when we can lean on the unlimited understanding of a faithful God? Many of the things that cause us the most heartache in life is the result of leaning to our own understanding.

This year, let's set aside our own understanding and lean totally on God. In doing so, we allow Him to direct our paths!

Psalms 37:5; Isaiah 26:3-4; Psalms 62:8

September 4

Daily Devotion for DESTINY:

Psalms 119:148 (English Standard Version) - My eyes are awake before the watches of the night, that I may meditate on your promise.

Happy Meditation Day! The bible is a book in which we may continually meditate but never exhaust all of its content. The same is true about the precepts and principles in the bible.

In our scripture today where the Psalmist lets us know that he wakes up early to engage in meditating on God's word. Could that be one of the reasons that he was a man after God's own heart? This is how the day in the life of a person that truly wants to reach their destination looks like.

This year, let's put God first by starting our day out with meditation and devotion. You will be so glad that you did!

Lamentations 2:19; Psalms 119:62; Luke 6:12

September 5

Daily Devotion for DESTINY:

II Corinthians 4:16 (English Standard Version) - **16** So we do not lose heart. Though our outer self[a] is wasting away, our inner self is being renewed day by day.

It is Transformation Day! If we are going to profit from our scripture today, we must first understand it. The outer man refers to our physical body. The wasting away of our outer man is most likely a reference to the fact that our fleshly bodies will eventually return to dust.

The good news is that as we meditate on God's word and transform our minds, our inner man is being renewed each day. What makes this amazing is that both processes are occurring at the same time.

This year, let's focus on the transformation of our inner man and our outer man will follow!

Colossians 3:10; Ephesians 3:16; Isaiah 40:29

September 6

Daily Devotion for DESTINY:

Ecclesiastes 2:26 (New International Version) - **26** To the person who pleases him, God gives wisdom, knowledge and happiness, but to the sinner he gives the task of gathering and storing up wealth to hand it over to the one who pleases God. This too is meaningless, a chasing after the wind.

It is Wisdom Day! We are not of ourselves naturally good, so when we choose to do good, it pleases God and He rewards us with knowledge, wisdom (the ability to apply knowledge) and happiness.

To the one who chooses NOT to do good, God gives the task of gathering up riches (without the wisdom and knowledge of how to use them and without any proper enjoyment of them) only to turn the riches over to the one who chooses to do good!

This year, let's choose to do good in the sight of God and allow Him to give us His wisdom and His knowledge and all of the benefits that accompany them!

Proverbs 13:22; Proverbs 28:8; James 3:17

September 7

Daily Devotion for DESTINY:

Psalms 116:17 (New International Version) - I will sacrifice a thank offering to you and call on the name of the Lord.

It is Thankful Day! There are some trials and tribulations that we go through that makes it very hard for us to be thankful. During these times, we can't seem to remember any of the times that God came through for us.

On the other hand, there is a praise that comes out of us during these times that causes God to turn His ear towards us. It is a "sacrifice of praise"! Such sacrifices are pleasing to God and causes Him to come to our rescue.

This year, let's not only be thankful while everything is going according to plan, but let's offer a sacrifice of thanksgiving even when we can't see our way through!

Psalms 50:14; Hebrews 13:15; Psalms 107:22

September 8

Daily Devotion for DESTINY:

John 20:27-29 (English Standard Version) - **7** Then he said to Thomas, "Put your finger here, and see my hands; and put out your hand and place it in my side. Do not disbelieve, but believe." **28** Thomas answered him, "My Lord and my God!" **29** Jesus said to him, "Have you believed because you have seen me? Blessed are those who have not seen and yet have believed."

Happy Faith Day! There is a very popular saying in the world today, "Seeing is believing"! Although this may hold true in some areas of our lives, we must make sure that this is not the standard that we apply to our walk with God.

As Christians, we believe the opposite when it comes to our faith. We do not walk by sight, we trust and believe in an almighty God. Jesus sent a blessing to those that believe without seeing.

This year, let's not have the Thomas kind of faith, but let's have faith that believes even (and especially) when we can't see!

I Peter 1:8; II Corinthians 5:7; Hebrews 11:1

September 9

Daily Devotion for DESTINY:

Matthew 24:42 (The Amplified bible, classic edition) - **42** Watch therefore [[a]give strict attention, be cautious and active], for you do not know in what kind of a day [[b]whether a near or remote one] your Lord is coming.

Christ's purpose for the advice in our scripture today was that He wanted us to keep the attitude of expectation of His return from generation through generations. He wanted us to know that this is an event that could happen at any time and must happen sometime.

The disciples asked Jesus what would be the signs of His return and the end of the age? Jesus talked about wars and rumors of wars, famines, earthquakes and false Christs; However, He told them that when they see these things happening, the end was Not yet.

In Matthew 24:14, Jesus told the disciples the only reliable predictor of the end of time as we know it. He said that when the Gospel of the Kingdom is proclaimed throughout the whole world as a testimony to all nations, THEN THE END WILL COME. The advanced technology that we now have (including social media) makes this possible. Are you ready?

Matthew 24:14; I Thessalonians 5:6; Matthew 24:44

September 10

Daily Devotion for DESTINY:

II Chronicles 7:14 (The Amplified Bible, classic edition) - **14** If My people, who are called by My name, shall humble themselves, pray, seek, crave, *and* require of necessity My face and turn from their wicked ways, then will I hear from heaven, forgive their sin, and heal their land.

Good morning! Today, many people are praying, but how many of us are repenting? I have heard our scripture for today quoted quite a bit in the last few days, but only a portion of it. We all agree that we need to pray; however, we must also humble ourselves, seek His face and turn from our wicked ways (repent)!

God's promises are conditional. If we want to receive the end result of the promise, we must meet ALL of the conditions connected to that promise.

Today (and every day), let's not only pray, but let's humble ourselves before the Lord, seek His face and repent for known and unknown sins and allow God to heal our land!

Isaiah 55:6-7; Proverbs 28:13; II Chronicles 6:27

September 11

Daily Devotion for DESTINY:

Psalms 77:12 (English Standard Version) - I will ponder all your work and meditate on your mighty deeds.

Happy Meditation Day! Our minds are important when it comes to learning God's will for our lives and following His will. Meditation is the most important tool we have to shape our minds, so we can comprehend what God is speaking to our spirits about our destiny.

Rick Warren made an awesome point in his book "The Purpose Driven Life" when he said, "If you know how to worry, you already know how to meditate". Worry is focusing (meditating) all of our thoughts on everything that could go wrong.

This year, let's turn worry into worship by meditating on God's word and everything that can and will go right!

Psalms 104:34; Psalms 119:15; Psalms 1:2

September 12

Daily Devotion for DESTINY:

I John 2:3-6 (English Standard Version) - **3** And by this we know that we have come to know him, if we keep his commandments. **4** Whoever says "I know him" but does not keep his commandments is a liar, and the truth is not in him, **5** but whoever keeps his word, in him truly the love of God is perfected. By this we may know that we are in him: **6** whoever says he abides in him ought to walk in the same way in which he walked.

It is Transformation Day! Our scripture today tells us how others will know that we have been transformed. God gives us the criteria to us to determine if we (and others that bear His name) are living a transformed life.

Why is this important? Because Matthew 5 tells us that once we are transformed, we are the salt of the earth and the light of the world. We are to season the earth with Christ like characteristics and be the light in a dark world.

This year, let's live the transformed life that God desires for us to live so that His will can be done on earth as it is in heaven.

John 15:10; I John 5:3; I John 3:19

September 13

Daily Devotion for DESTINY:

Isaiah 5:21 (English Standard Version) - Woe to those who are wise in their own eyes, and shrewd in their own sight!

It is Wisdom Day! This warning comes to those who feel that they are already wise enough and do not feel that they need to listen to others. Our Savior requires us to be meek, humble and most of all, teachable.

Most of us at some point in our lives have been guilty of being wise in our own eyes. All true wisdom comes from God. James 1:5 lets us know that if we lack wisdom, we can ask God and it shall be given unto him.

This year, lets transition from being wise in our own eyes to asking God for His wisdom and being wise in God's eyes!

Proverbs 3:7; Romans 12:16; Proverbs 26:12

September 14

Daily Devotion for DESTINY:

I Thessalonians 5:18 (English Standard Version) - **18** give thanks in all circumstances; for this is the will of God in Christ Jesus for you.

It is Thankful Day! As we embark upon our journey of discovering our purpose (the reason that we were born), we can rest assured knowing that there is one assignment that we all have in common.

It does not matte4r where your destiny leads you, God has challenged us to give thanks in ALL circumstances. This is His will for all of us. He knew that we would encounter many trials and tribulations (circumstances) on our way to our destination, so He gave us the formula for a successful journey.

In the coming days and weeks, let's give thanks through our circumstances. This will put you in the safest place in the whole wide world...God's perfect will!!

Ephesians 5:20, Philippians 4:6; Colossians 3:17

September 15

Daily Devotion for DESTINY:

John 11:40 (Amplified Bible, classic edition) - **40** Jesus said to her, Did I not tell you *and* [a]promise you that if you would believe *and* rely on Me, you would see the glory of God?

Happy Faith Day! Our scripture today lets us know that if we believe (have faith in) God, we will see the glory of God. What better way to see God's glory than to complete the assignment that he has given to us.

You will know if the assignment that you are pursuing came from God. A God-given assignment always go beyond our ability and capability; therefore, we must have faith that God will help us complete our assignment.

This year, let's build our faith so that when God reveals our assignment to us, we can get on it because we trust in God to help us accomplish it!

John 1:14; II Corinthians 3:18; Psalms 90:16

September 16

Daily Devotion for DESTINY:

Joshua 1:9 (English Standard Version) - 9 Have I not commanded you? Be strong and courageous. Do not be frightened, and do not be dismayed, for the Lord your God is with you wherever you go."

Many people today are stepping out of their comfort zones and moving into their assigned place in God. For some, this move includes a change in geographical locations and for others, it is a move only in their Spiritual lives (i.e. from fear to faith).

As with our scripture today. God is calling us away from the dead things in our comfort zone to the living things ahead of us that He has prepared. He just wants us to trust Him to direct our path. All He asks is that we acknowledge Him during our decision-making process and He will lead and guide us.

I want to encourage you today to obey the prompting of the Lord that is encouraging you to step out of your comfort zone. As God was with Moses and Joshua, so will He be with you!

Genesis 28:15; Jeremiah 1:7-8; Deuteronomy 20:1

September 17

Daily Devotion for DESTINY:

Isaiah 55:11(The Amplified Bible, classic edition) - **1** So shall My word be that goes forth out of My mouth: it shall not return to Me void [without producing any effect, useless], but it shall accomplish that which I please *and* purpose, and it shall prosper in the thing for which I sent it.

As each one of us prepares to go to church this morning to receive inspiration and instruction, I want to encourage you to ask the Lord to help you apply the word that you hear to your specific destiny.

Part of the job of the Holy Spirit is to help us rightly divide the word and apply it to our lives. Many different people can hear the same word and it will mean something different to each one because God's word is tailor made just for us. Who better to ask how the word applies to us than the One who made us?

God sent His word before we were born and it will not return unto Him void. Today (and every day) let's apply the Word of God that we hear to our lives!

Matthew 24:25; Isaiah 46:10; I Corinthians 1:18

September 18

Daily Devotion for DESTINY:

Jeremiah 1:5 (The Amplified Bible, classic edition) - **5** Before I formed you in the womb I knew [and] approved of you [as My chosen instrument], and before you were born I separated *and* set you apart, consecrating you; [and] I appointed you as a prophet to the nations.

Happy Meditation Day! Now that I think that we understand what biblical meditation is and how important it is to our spiritual walk, I am going to share some areas of our lives that we can meditate on during Meditation Days.

This week, let's start at the very beginning of each one of our lives; the reason that we were born. Our scripture today lets us know that God set us apart to be used by Him in a specific area of ministry. This is called purpose. Jeremiah's purpose was to be a Prophet to the nations.

What is your purpose? As you meditate on that question today, ask God to reveal to you the reason that you were born. Ask Him to make it so clear to you, that there will not be any room for doubt as you pursue your purpose. I promise you that He will do it!

Isaiah 49:1; Romans 8:29; Luke 1:76

September 19

Daily Devotion for DESTINY:

Romans 12:1-2 (English Standard Version) - **12** I appeal to you therefore, brothers,[a] by the mercies of God, to present your bodies as a living sacrifice, holy and acceptable to God, which is your spiritual worship. [b] **2** Do not be conformed to this world,[c]but be transformed by the renewal of your mind, that by testing you may discern what is the will of God, what is good and acceptable and perfect.

It is Transformation Day! Our scripture today is urging us to give God true worship by presenting our bodies as a living sacrifice, holy and pleasing to Him. We learned last week that God honors our sacrifices.

The bible goes on to tell us not to conform to the ways of this world but transform our minds so that we can conform to the ways of God. The only way that we can live holy before a holy God is with a transformed mind.

As you continue to meditate on God's word, you will find that a transformation is taking place in your mind. It is only then that we will be able to discern God's will for our lives.

Romans 6:13; Ephesians 4:1; II Corinthians 4:16

September 24

Daily Devotion for DESTINY:

Ecclesiastes 3:1 (English Standard Version) - **3** For everything there is a season, and a time for every matter under heaven:

It is very important to discover your assignment and purpose in life because the above scripture lets us know that there is a time and a season for everything. We do not want to miss our season.

We must keep our ears open to the voice of the Lord and allow Him to order not only our steps, but our timing to make those steps. When we move in God's timing, we will meet the provisions that He has made for us. These provisions include divine connections, divine appointments and divine favor.

This year, let's make sure that we move in God's timing and allow Him to prepare the way for our arrival!

Matthew 16:3; Proverbs 15:23; Ecclesiastes 8:5-6

September 25

Daily Devotion for DESTINY:

Psalms 119:15 (English Standard Version) - I will meditate on your precepts and fix my eyes on your ways,

Happy Meditation Day!I want to encourage you to meditate on determining what season you are in right now.

God spoke to my heart that there is a season for everything and we must determine what season we are in so that we can walk in the provisions for that season. This is vital as we journey towards our destiny.

Today and every day, let's focus our meditation on our time and season and walk therein.

Psalms 119:48; Psalms 119:6; Psalms 119:23

September 26

Daily Devotion for DESTINY

II Corinthians 4:8-9 (English Standard Version) - **8** We are afflicted in every way, but not crushed; perplexed, but not driven to despair; **9** persecuted, but not forsaken; struck down, but not destroyed;

It is Transformation Day! I feel strong that in the midst of all of the madness going on in our lives, God is doing a work in us. As I sat in church a few days ago, I heard Pastor Riva Tims say something that struck my spirit and ignited a determination in me like I have never felt before.

She said that we were created for adversity! Do not think it strange when we encounter adversity. This is what causes us to transform into the person that God had in mind when He created us.!

This year, let's allow the adversity that we face make us better instead of bitter. This is true transformation!

James 1:2-4; I Peter 4:12-14; II Corinthians 12:10

September 27

Daily Devotion for DESTINY:

Proverbs 19:20 (English Standard Version) - Listen to advice and accept instruction that you may gain wisdom in the future.

It is Wisdom Day! We are living in a time when we have to be willing to accept correction if we are going to reach our destiny. Our scripture today tells us that wise men (and women) hear counsel, receive instruction and accept discipline.

I know that this is not a popular word in these times, but it is a very necessary word. We must be open to receive correction whether it be directly from God, or from the vessels that God sends to us.

This year, let's be wise and not only hear counsel and receive instruction, but let's also accept correction and move forward!

Proverbs 12:15; Proverbs 1:8; Proverbs 4:1

September 28

Daily Devotion for DESTINY:

Romans 6:23 (The Amplified Bible, classic edition) -**23** For the wages which sin pays is death, but the [bountiful] free gift of God is eternal life through (in union with) Jesus Christ our Lord.

It is Thankful Day! The term wages signify the reward that we get when we render service. It is something that is earned. The wages of our sins are death.

In spite of our sanctification through Christ, we still have not earned eternal life. It is a gift of God's grace. Today and every day, I am thankful that God did not pay me what I earned (death), but He gave me what I did not deserve (eternal life).

This year, let's honor God's grace to us by thanking Him for His gift of eternal life that He so willingly gives to those who receives Him in their hearts!

John 3:36; James 1:15'; Matthew 25:46

September 29

Daily Devotion for DESTINY:

Numbers 14:11 (The Amplified Bible, classic edition) - **11** And the Lord said to Moses, How long will this people provoke (spurn, despise) Me? And how long will it be before they believe Me [trusting in, relying on, clinging to Me], for all the signs which I have performed among them?

Happy Faith Day! Our scripture today is the definition of Israel's sin. They murmured and complained, and they simply did not believe God even after all the miracles that He had performed for them.

I can hear these same questions echoing in my spirit. How long will we despise the ways of the Lord? How long will it be before we trust Him with our heart and our lives? We grieve the Lord when we walk in unbelief (which is the opposite of faith). Hebrews 11:6 lets us know that without faith, it is impossible to please Him.

This year, lets determine in our hearts that we will have faith in God, not only for ourselves but for our loved ones and everyone else whose destiny depends on us making it to our destination!

Psalms 106:24; John 12:37; Psalms 78:32

September 30

Daily Devotion for DESTINY:

Proverbs 3:5-6 (The Amplified Bible, classic edition) - **5** Lean on, trust in, *and* be confident in the Lord with all your heart *and mind* and do not rely on your own insight *or* understanding.

6 In all your ways know, recognize, *and* acknowledge Him, and He will direct *and* make straight *and* plain your paths.

We have been talking a lot about walking in the will of God to our destiny. How do we know the specifics of the will of God for us? For the next few days, I am going to discuss a few indicators that we can use to determine God's specific will concerning our destiny.

The first thing we must do is surrender our will to God. We cannot seek God's will and set boundaries in the back of our minds on what we are willing to follow and what we are not willing to follow. Also, we must obey what we already know to be the will of God. Much of God's will is already written in His word (the bible). We are seeking Him for the specifics of our lives that are not written in the bible. For instance, what is the next step in my career? What is the next step in my ministry?

This year, it is very important that we hear the voice of God concerning His will for our lives. Stay tuned as we learn how to do this!

Mark 3:35; Hebrews 10:36; John 9:31(b)

October

¹⁶ *All Scripture is God-breathed and is useful for teaching, rebuking, correcting and training in righteousness,*

II Timothy 3:16 (NIV)

October 1

Daily Devotion for DESTINY:

I John 2:17 (English Standard Version) - **17** And the world is passing away along with its desires, but whoever does the will of God abides forever.

I hope everyone enjoyed Your devotions and are now empowered to make it through this week. We are going to continue our discussion on how to discover the will of God for our lives.

God has raised up people and placed them in our lives for the sole purpose of speaking to our destiny. They are called Divine connections. Ask God to reveal these people to you. Some may just give you Godly council and some may actually be in the position to open God-ordained doors for you.

This year, pay close attention to the people that comes across your path. Hebrews 13:2 warns us to be careful how we treat strangers; We may be entertaining Angles (Divine connections) unaware.

Mark 3:35; Hebrews 10:36; Colossians 1:9

October 2

Daily Devotion for DESTINY:

Psalms 139:15-16 (New King James Version) - **15** My frame was not hidden from You, When I was made in secret, and skillfully wrought in the lowest parts of the earth.**16** Your eyes saw my substance, being yet unformed. And in Your book, they all were written, The days fashioned for me, When *as yet there were* none of them.

Happy Meditation Day! As we continue our study on how to discover God's will for our lives, let us spend today meditating on our scripture. This will help us understand the importance of finding our assignment in life and reaching our destination.

God had all of our days planned before we were born. He was not surprised by our entrance into the earth. Our physical features, our personalities and everything else about us was specifically designed by God for a specific purpose.

As we seek God's will for our lives, let us celebrate who we are. Psalms 139:14 lets us know that we were fearfully and wonderfully made! This means you!!

Job 10:8-11; Malachi 3:16; Psalms 139:14

October 3

Daily Devotion for DESTINY:

Ephesians 5:17 (The Amplified Bible, classic edition) - **17** Therefore do not be vague *and* thoughtless *and* foolish but understanding *and* firmly grasping what the will of the Lord is.

It is Transformation Day! We are going to continue our study on finding and following God's will for our lives. We can't assume that God's will is going to automatically come to pass in our lives. It does not. We have to make a conscious effort to find His will for us.

Once we realize that we are responsible for finding God's will for us, the next step is to seek Him for it. Jeremiah 29:12-13 tells us how to seek God for His will. It says that we will find God (and His will for our lives) when we seek Him with all of our heart. Transformation is truly a heart thing!

How are we going to build God's Kingdom without knowing what part that we are destined to play? Refuse to live another day not knowing the will of God for your life!

Jeremiah 29:12-13; Colossians 1:9; I Peter 4:2

October 4

Daily Devotion for DESTINY:

I Peter 4:10 (The Amplified Bible, classic edition) - **10** As each of you has received a gift (a particular spiritual talent, a gracious divine endowment), employ it for one another as [befits] good trustees of God's many-sided grace [faithful stewards of the [a]extremely diverse powers and gifts granted to Christians by unmerited favor].

On this Wisdom Day, we are going to discuss another way to discover God's will for your life. A very important step in discerning God's will is to pay attention to how you are wired.

By this I mean, pay attention to your likes, dislikes and passions. Most of all, pay attention to your gifts. God has wired us specifically according to our destiny. God's will for us will always be directly related to the gifts that He has given you. You will automatically be good at whatever God has called you to do.

There is no one else in this world that can achieve completely what God has created you to do. Take this time to discover what that is. Someone's life depends on it!!!

Mark 10:45; Matthew 25:44; Hebrews 6:10

October 5

Daily Devotion for DESTINY:

Mark 13:31 (English Standard Version) - **31** Heaven and earth will pass away, but my words will not pass away.

This is Thankful Day and today I want to thank God for uncovering the deep things concerning His will for us! We are still learning how to know what God's will is for our lives

Our scripture lets us know that Heaven and Earth will pass away, but what God has said concerning our destiny will not pass away. Even if we choose not to walk in our destiny, it is still God's desire for us.

This year, pay attention to the subtle clues that God gives you concerning your destiny. He wants us to seek and find. Enjoy your journey!

Matthew 5:18; Luke 21:33; Isaiah 40:8

October 6

Daily Devotion for DESTINY:

I Timothy 4:10 (English Standard Version) - **10** For to this end we toil and strive,[a] because we have our hope set on the living God, who is the Savior of all people, especially of those who believe.

Happy Faith Day! We are still taking about learning and following God's will for our lives. As I scripture for today says; to this end we toil and strive. What end? We strive to reach our destiny! The other day, we learned that we should pay attention to what we are good at. I wanted to issue a warning along this line.

Although it is very, very important to pay attention to what you are good at; be very careful not to assume that because you are good at something, it must be your destiny. For example, if you happen to be a great public speaker, it does not necessarily mean that your destiny is a Pastor.

Many times God calls us to do what is beyond our natural ability so that we will be dependent up Him. As we seek Him, He will let us know if the thing that we are good at is because it is our destiny, or just a talent to enjoy.

Psalms 84:12; Nahum 1:7; Jeremiah 17:7

October 7

Daily Devotion for DESTINY:

Philippians 4:7 (English Standard Version) - **7** And the peace of God, which surpasses all understanding, will guard your hearts and your minds in Christ Jesus.

I want to wrap up our discussion on learning God's will for our lives with our scripture for today. I want to encourage you to above all else, follow peace. Both the absence and the presence of peace will let you know if you are on the same page as God concerning His will for your life.

Colossians 3:15 in the Amplified bible lets us know that peace acts as an umpire in our lives. The umpire in a baseball game makes the final decision on any questions that arise during the course of the game. So it is with peace.

Let's begin today allowing peace to guide us through the decisions that we must make each day as well as lead us to our destiny. Peace comes from a mind aligned with God because He is the Author of peace.

Colossians 3:15; John 14:27; Isaiah 26:3

October 8

Daily Devotion for DESTINY:

Luke 2:52 (International Standard Version) - **52** Meanwhile, Jesus kept on growing wiser and more mature, and in favor with God and his fellow man.

We have been preparing this entire year to discover and walk out our God-ordained destiny. This morning, I want to help you understand the importance of preparation. Our scripture today picks up after Jesus had gone to Jerusalem with His family for the annual Passover Festival. After the festival, Jesus' family had been traveling a full day before they realized that Jesus was not with them.

They went back to Jerusalem and found Jesus three days later in the temple amongst the teachers. He went home with His parents and we do not hear anything else about him until 18 years later when John baptized Jesus at the age of 30. What was Jesus doing during those "Silent years"? He was preparing for His ministry by growing wiser and in favor with God AND man.

If Jesus, who is our ultimate example had to prepare for ministry, so must we. He prepared 30 years for a ministry that was to only last 3 years! Let's spend the remainder of the year preparing for where God is taking us!

Luke 2:40; I Samuel 2:26; Romans 14:18

October 9

Daily Devotion for DESTINY:

I Peter 2:9 (The Amplified Bible, classic edition) - **9** But you are a chosen race, a royal priesthood, a dedicated nation, [God's] own [a]purchased, special people, that you may set forth the wonderful deeds *and* display the virtues and perfections of Him Who called you out of darkness into His marvelous light.

Happy Meditation Day! Today I would like for us all to meditate on who we are once we accept Jesus into our lives. If you have not already done so, please read today's scripture because it tells us exactly who we are in Christ. Up until about 6 months ago, for many years, I kept having a re-occurring dream that my wallet (and sometimes purse) was getting stolen.

After several of these dreams, I got the feeling that the Lord was trying to say something to me, so I asked Him why did I keep having these dreams? He asked me what do I keep in my wallet (purse)? For some reason, the first thing that came to mind was my license. Our license is a form of identity. I could hear the still, small voice of God saying that satan is trying to steal your identity.

It is very important that we know who we are in Christ because once we do, we cannot be stopped. A person who knows who they are in God is one of the enemy's greatest threats. Today (and everyday) let's meditate on who we are in God and allow Him to speak to us concerning our identity. There are so many things that He wants to say to you!!!

Deuteronomy 7:6; Ephesians 5:8-11; John 15:15

October 10

Daily Devotion for DESTINY:

Philippians 1:6 (The Amplified Bible, classic edition) - **6** And I am convinced *and* sure of this very thing, that He Who began a good work in you will continue until the day of Jesus Christ [right up to the time of His return], developing [that good work] *and* perfecting *and bringing* it to full completion in you.

It is Transformation Day! I think that it is important for us to realize that once we decide to transform our minds to line up with our decision to accept Jesus into our hearts; we sign up for a life-long process.

As we do what we can do in terms of our transformation, God will do what we cannot do. We must be committed to this process if we are going to reach our destiny. Every step of our Christian walk depends on our reliance on God.

This year, let's make up in our minds that we will work on our transformation until the day that we go to be with Jesus. He will be with us every step of the way!

Philippians 2:13; Ephesians 4:12; I Corinthians 1:8

October 11

Daily Devotion for DESTINY:

Proverbs 1:23 (The Amplified Bible, classic edition) - **23** If you will turn (repent) *and* give heed to my reproof, behold, I [[a]Wisdom] will pour out my spirit upon you, I will make my words known to you.

It is Wisdom Day! There are many benefits to walking in wisdom. We have explored some of those benefits, but over the next few weeks on Wisdom Day, we are going to focus on just a few of these benefits.

One very important benefit of walking in wisdom is that it reveals to us what God is speaking to our spirit. We are living in the information age and with access to so much information, it is sometimes hard to hear what God is saying. We choose what information system we allow to mold our thinking and our actions. We need God's wisdom to make that choice because not all information is bad, but it may not be for you.

God is always speaking. This year, let's fine tune our ability to hear Him by walking in wisdom.

Psalms 37:30; I Corinthians 1:26; James 3:17

October 12

Daily Devotion for DESTINY:

I Thessalonians 5:16-18 (English Standard Version) - **16** Rejoice always, **17** pray without ceasing, **18** give thanks in all circumstances; for this is the will of God in Christ Jesus for you.

It is Thankful Day! We have another opportunity to focus on the goodness of God and thank Him for all that He has done for us. Many of God's commandments are beyond our ability to obey in our flesh, so we must rely on the Holy Spirit to help us obey them.

So it is with the three commandments in our scripture for today. Even though we will probably not perfect these commandments in this life, we should be working towards that goal not just on Thankful Days, but every day of the year.

Thankfulness will become a habit when we trust God. Begin to build your trust in God and you will be on the path of perfecting these commandments.

Ephesians 5:20; Philippians 4:6; Colossians 3:17

October 13

Daily Devotion for DESTINY:

James 1:3-4 (English Standard Version) - **3** for you know that the testing of your faith produces steadfastness.**4** And let steadfastness have its full effect, that you may be perfect and complete, lacking in nothing.

Happy Faith Day! There is a deep connection between our daily life and our spiritual growth. What I mean is that God often uses the trials and tribulations that we go through in our daily lives to increase our faith.

We know that God is a God of purpose and everything that He does has a purpose. The purpose of testing our faith is to produce patience and patience is a necessary element of spiritual growth.

This year, when our faith is tested, count it as joy and submit to God know that He is using it for our maturity!

Romans 5:3-4; I Peter 1:7; II Corinthians 4:17

October 14

Daily Devotion for DESTINY:

I John 2:16-17 (English Standard Version) - **16** For all that is in the world—the desires of the flesh and the desires of the eyes and pride of life[a]—is not from the Father but is from the world.**17** And the world is passing away along with its desires, but whoever does the will of God abides forever.

I saw a post from a group that I belong to that I had to share because I have experienced this and I know it to be true. The post reads, "The most dangerous thing about going outside of God's will to get what you want is that you will have to stay out to keep it."

Take it from me, there is absolutely nothing in this world worth going outside of God's will to get. I thank God that I had the opportunity to get back in His will before it was too late!

If you find yourself outside of God's will today, I encourage you to run (not walk) back to God and allow Him to give you the desires of His heart.

Genesis 3:6; Romans 13:14; Galatians 5:17

October 15

Daily Devotion for DESTINY:

Exodus 33:19 (The Amplified Bible, classic edition) - **17** And the Lord said to Moses, I will do this thing also that you have asked, for you have found favor, loving-kindness, *and* mercy in My sight and I know you personally *and* by name.

God formed a special relationship with the children of Israel after He brought them out of slavery into Egypt. By the time we get to our scripture for today, the children of Israel had stumbled. They hurt God in the worst way by worshipping a golden calf. God had decided that they can still go to the promise land, but instead of going with them, He would send an angel.

When God told Moses that His presence would not be with them as they traveled through the wilderness, Moses interceded for the people. This is where our scripture today come in. Because of the favor that Moses had with God, He changed His mind. Even though the journey through the wilderness was treacherous, God was with them.

This year, let's step into the favor of God in every area of our lives. It is the favor of God that will open doors for us!

Genesis 19:21; Genesis 6:8; Genesis 19:19

October 16

Daily Devotion for DESTINY:

Psalms 119:11 (English Standard Version) - I have stored up your word in my heart, that I might not sin against you.

Happy Meditation Day! What does it mean to hide the word in your heart? It means to hear it, read it, mix it with faith and store it up for future use. In other words, hiding the word of God in your heart means to meditate on it.

The word of God is the one most powerful weapons that we have to fight sin with. We see in Matthew 4 how Jesus used the word to defeat the devil and so must we.

This year, let's meditate on the word of God until it is hidden in our hearts, then go out and defeat the devil on every level!

Psalms 37:31; Psalms 40:8; Luke 2:19

October 17

Daily Devotion for DESTINY:

Romans 8:5-6 (English Standard Version) - **5** For those who live according to the flesh set their minds on the things of the flesh, but those who live according to the Spirit set their minds on the things of the Spirit. **6** For to set the mind on the flesh is death, but to set the mind on the Spirit is life and peace.

It is Transformation Day! God often gives us choices. He made us free-will agents with hopes that we would choose to live for Him. Our scripture today lets us know the reward that we receive when we choose to live for God as well as the consequences when we choose to live for our flesh.

We choose whether to transform our minds so that we can live according to the Spirit, or we choose to set our minds on temporal things (things according the flesh) and live according to our flesh.

We are living in a time when our decisions could be a matter of life or death. Transform your mind and choose life!

Galatians 5:19-25; I Corinthians 2:14; John 3:6

October 18

Daily Devotion for DESTINY:

Proverbs 3:35 (English Standard Version) - The wise will inherit honor, but fools get[a] disgrace.

Word for Wisdom Day! Our decisions will earn us either glory or shame. There are consequences for every decision that we make. We will not always see the consequences right away, but they cannot be avoided.

Wise men (and women) make decisions based on the word of God. Foolish men (and women) make decisions based on feelings, thoughts, popular opinion, traditions and habits.

This year, lets choose to be wise and inherit the earth rather than choosing to be foolish and inherit disgrace.

Daniel 12:2-3; Isaiah 65:13-15; I Samuel 2:30

October 19

Daily Devotion for DESTINY:

Psalms 116:12 (English Standard Version) - What shall I render to the Lord for all his benefits to me?

It is Thankful Day! Even though much of Psalms was written by David, it is not clear who wrote Psalms 116, but it is very clear that the author was giving thanks to God for delivering him from a near-death experience.

This psalm was written some time after the author's brush with death. As the psalmist reflected on this experience, he begins to tell the things that he learned about God and asked what he could give to God for all that God had done for him. He decided to give God a thankful heart!

We may not have had a near-death experience, but we can all testify to the goodness of God and give God a thankful heart in return for all of His benefits toward us!

I Corinthians 6:20; Romans 12:1; Psalms 103:2

October 20

Daily Devotion for DESTINY:

Romans 15:13 (The Amplified Bible, classic edition) - **13** May the God of your hope so fill you with all joy and peace in believing [through the experience of your faith] that by the power of the Holy Spirit you may abound *and* be overflowing (bubbling over) with hope.

Happy Faith Day! Our scripture today is a prayer that Paul prayed for the believers. To some degree, we all fall short of experiencing joy and peace in its entirety. Could this be because our faith is not entirely in God?

We can all benefit from thinking about these qualities (joy and peace) and how we can grow in them. As we build our faith in God, we will find that we will grow in joy and in peace.

It is very important that we make sure that we walk in peace. As we learned several days ago, peace is our umpire in our journey towards our destiny!

Romans 14:17; Romans 12:12; I Peter 1:8

October 21

Daily Devotion for DESTINY:

Psalms 46:10 (English Standard Version) - "Be still and know that I am God. I will be exalted among the nations, I will be exalted in the earth!"

For those of us who have decided to discover our purpose and have begun our journey towards our destiny, you are probably experiencing many new things. Most likely, God is beginning to speak to your spirit in His still, small voice.

You may be starting to become aware of you likes and dislikes concerning your personality and wondering how they fit into your purpose. Those are the people that this devotion is directed to. God is not trying to hide His will from you. He wants us to seek Him because our preparation for our purpose is wrapped in our journey.

This year, allow God to speak to you and stand still until His will is clear. He will not leave you hanging!

Psalms 37:7; Exodus 14:14; Psalms 62:5

October 22

Daily Devotion for DESTINY:

Ecclesiastes 3:1 (The Amplified Bible, classic edition) - To everything there is a season, and a time for every matter *or purpose* under heaven:

Good morning! As we prepare to go to church this morning, I want to pose a question to you. What season are you in as it relates to your destiny: Our scripture today lets us know that to everything there is a time and a season.

We learned in our Daily Devotion a few days ago to be still while we are determining what season we are in. Today, I would like to talk to those who are clear on what direction the Lord wants you to go. It is time to step out on what God spoke to you concerning your destiny!

This year, we do not want to miss the timing of God because the provisions that He has prepared are waiting for us to arrive. Remember, if there is no doubt, the time is Now!!!

Ecclesiastes 8:5-6; Genesis 8:22; Habakkuk 2:3

October 23

Daily Devotion for DESTINY:

Psalms 31:15 (English Standard Version) - My times are in your hand; rescue me from the hand of my enemies and from my persecutors!

Happy Meditation Day! I was so moved by our daily devotion yesterday, that I would like for us to sit right there today. As we meditate on the word of God today, lets allow God to speak to us concerning what season we are in as far as our personal purpose.

There have been times in my life when I have missed the season (and provisions that go along with the season) and I had to wait for that season to come back around. I am still waiting on some opportunities to come back around.

It that is your story, do not fret! These opportunities will come back around and this time you will have no doubt and you will step out!!!

Proverbs 15:23; Romans 13:11; Daniel 2:21

October 24

Daily Devotion for DESTINY:

I John 3:2 (New International Version) - **2** Dear friends, now we are children of God, and what we will be has not yet been made known. But we know that when Christ appears,[a] we shall be like him, for we shall see him as he is.

It is Transformation Day! We are in a constant state of transformation as long as we are on this earth. Our scripture today describes the ultimate transformation that the Children of God has to look forward to. This is the transformation that will take place when Christ appears.

A while back, I touched on the fact that children normally bear some type of resemblance to their parents. Since flesh and blood cannot inherit the Kingdom, the scripture (I Corinthians 15:53 lets us know that we will be transformed from mortal to immortality.

This year, let's begin our earthly transformation so that we can participate in the ultimate transformation when Jesus returns.

II Corinthians 3:18; Colossians 3:4; I Corinthians 15:53

October 25

Daily Devotion for DESTINY:

Proverbs 2:6 (The Amplified Bible, classic edition) -**6** For the Lord gives skillful *and* Godly Wisdom; from His mouth come knowledge and understanding.

It is Wisdom Day! Many of the situations that we find ourselves in and many of the things that we deal with are not necessarily because of the enemy. It is because of our choices. We need to access the wisdom of God to choose the right friends, make the right choices and move in God's timing.

Each time we make a choice outside of God's wisdom, we set the course of our lives back. Abraham made the decision to help God fulfill His promise and Abraham impregnated his hand maiden rather than wait on God. This choice delayed the child of promise by several years.

Beginning today, lets decide that our steps will be ordered by the wisdom of God and we will follow those orders!

Isaiah 54:13; I Kings 3:12; Psalms 119:98

October 26

Daily Devotion for DESTINY:

I Thessalonians 5:18 (The Amplified Bible, classic edition) - **18** Thank [God] in everything [no matter what the circumstances may be, be thankful and give thanks], for this is the will of God for you [who are] in Christ Jesus [the Revealer and Mediator of that will].

Welcome to Thankful Day! There are many benefits to being thankful, both spiritually and naturally. Today, I want to address some of the natural benefits. According to Dr. Robert Emmons, clinical trials indicate that gratitude lowers your blood pressure, improves immune function and facilitates more efficient sleep.

A recent study from the University of California School of Medicine found that people who were more grateful had better heart health (specifically, less inflammation and healthier heart rhythms) than those who were less grateful.

This year, lets pump up our Thanksgiving to God. It is part of His health care plan for us!

Hebrews 13:15; Ephesians 5:20; Philippians 4:6

October 27

Daily Devotion for DESTINY:

Isaiah 40:31 (New International Version) - but those who hope in the Lord will renew their strength. They will soar on wings like eagles; they will run and not grow weary, they will walk and not be faint.

Happy Faith Day! God knew that we would struggle with unbelief; therefore, He gave us reassuring words throughout the entire bible.

When you begin to doubt, refer to these scriptures and know that God will be there to strengthen you.

Our scripture today tells us that if our hope (faith) is in God, He will renew our strength during those times when we are struggling with unbelief. When we wait on the Lord with a spirit of expectation, He will always come through.

This year, lets renew our faith like the eagles whose feathers are renewed during its old age and run towards our destiny!

II Corinthians 4:16; Lamentations 3:25-26; Galatians 6:9

October 28

Daily Devotion for DESTINY:

I Peter 1:24-25 (The Amplified Bible, classic edition) -**24** For all flesh (mankind) is like grass, and all its glory (honor) like [the] flower of grass. The grass withers and the flower drops off, **25** But the Word of the Lord ([a]divine instruction, the Gospel) endures forever. And this Word is the good news which was preached to you.

As I was preparing to look up the scripture for our Daily Devotion for DESTINY today, I saw the verse of the day on Bible gateway and I knew that this was our scripture for today. I immediately heard in my spirit, "What are you focusing on"?

The verse for today lets us know that our flesh is like grass. If we refuse to feed the flesh; just like grass, it will wither away and the flower will drop off. On the other hand, if we water our spirits; just like grass, our spirit will continue to grow and become strong.

This year, lets focus less on our flesh and more on our spirits and continue to blossom in the things of God.

Isaiah 40:8; Matthew 5:18; Psalms 103:15

October 29

Daily Devotion for DESTINY:

Proverbs 20:5 (The Amplified Bible, classic edition) - **5** Counsel in the heart of man is like water in a deep well, but a man of understanding draws it out.

It takes skill to discover what others really think. What a wise man (woman) thinks can help you succeed. Our scripture compares the contents in the heart of man to a deep well. It takes a great deal of labor to bring the water to the surface. Many will look elsewhere for easier water.

Only a man (woman) with similar skills will have the ability and patience to extract the personal plans and opinions out of a wise man. True wise men (and women) are Godly and sober and not willing to speak until asked. Good counsel from wise advisors are necessary for our success.

This year, lets purpose in our hearts to seek out the wise counsel that God has provided for each one of us.

Proverbs 18:4; I Corinthians 2:11; Psalms 64:6

October 30

Daily Devotion for DESTINY

Hebrews 5:14 (English Standard Version) - **14** But solid food is for the mature, for those who have their powers of discernment trained by constant practice to distinguish good from evil.

Happy Meditation Day! When babies are born and for a while after, they can only consume milk. They cannot process nor digest anything beyond milk. In the same way, a new Christian can only process simple spiritual matters. This is not a problem because we want them to be able to process and digest according to their ability to do so.

It becomes a problem when a person remains in spiritual infancy many years after accepting Jesus as Lord and Savior. At this point, we should have grown enough to be able to process and digest solid food (The Word of God).

Let's take time on this Meditation Day to assess where we are on our spiritual timeline and making sure that we are receiving the proper nutrition for our spiritual age; whether it be milk or solid food.

I Corinthians 2:14-15; Philippians 1:9-10; Ephesians 4:13

October 31

Daily Devotion for DESTINY:

II Timothy 1:7 (New King James Version) - **7** For God has not given us a spirit of fear, but of power and of love and of a sound mind.

It is Transformation Day! A sound mind requires constant transformation. When our minds are guarded by the Word of God, there is not room left for fear. When we are feeding our minds the Word of God, it shields us from the arrows of the enemy.

It is important for us to understand this during our transformation because the enemy will try to assault us mentally and emotionally to hinder the progress that we are making.

This year, when the devil tries to convince you that you are losing your mind, remind him that God has not given you the spirit of fear, but of power, love and a SOUND mind!

I John 4:18; John 14:27; Luke 8:35

November

"I the LORD search the heart
and examine the mind,
to reward each person according to their conduct,
according to what their deeds deserve."

Jeremiah 17:10 (NIV)

November 1

Daily Devotion for DESTINY:

Proverbs 6:6-8 (English Standard Version) - Go to the ant, O sluggard consider her ways, and be wise. Without having any chief, officer, or ruler, she prepares her bread in summer and gathers her food in harvest.

It is Wisdom Day! A wise man (and woman) is diligent in business. We can all learn something from the ant both for our spiritual life as well as our natural life. Every day we should gather the Word of God and store it in our hearts for future use.

Our scripture today is a warning against laziness. The and had no leader and they gather their food in the summer, so that they will have food to eat in the winter. We have to be wise and store up for the future because the natural temptation is to spend as soon as it becomes available.

This year, let's be wise and store up (both spiritually and naturally) for our future.

Proverbs 30:25; Proverbs 20:4; Proverbs 10:5

November 2

Daily Devotion for DESTINY:

I Chronicles 16:34 (The Amplified Bible, classic edition) - **34** O give thanks to the Lord, for He is good; for His mercy *and* loving-kindness endure forever!

It is Thankful Day! Not only that, but we have entered the month where many people focus turns towards being thankful. It is very easy during this time of year to get overwhelmed with all of the tasks and activities that accompany the Holidays that we forget what is really important.

I challenge you to take a few moments out of each day for the remainder of the year and just thank God for His grace and mercy that has kept you up to this point. Many people that started off are no longer here, but we are! That is reason enough to praise our God!

This year, lets show God that we are thankful for everything that He has done and continues to do for us!!!

Ezra 3:11; Psalms 106:1; Psalms 118:1

November 3

Daily Devotion for DESTINY:

II Corinthians 4:18 (Amplified Bible, classic edition) - **18** Since we consider *and* look not to the things that are seen but to the things that are unseen; for the things that are visible are temporal (brief and fleeting), but the things that are invisible are deathless *and everlasting.*

Happy Faith Day! As human beings, it is natural for us to focus on things that we can see. As spiritual beings, we are required to walk by faith and not by sight; therefore, focusing on things that we cannot see.

The things that we see are the circumstances of our present life. The things which are not seen are the objects of our faith. The circumstances of our present life have an expiration date; however, the objects of our faith are eternal.

This year, let's do as Colossians 3:2 tells us and set our minds on things above (eternal) and not on things on this earth (temporal).

Colossians 3:2; II Corinthians 5:7; Hebrews 11:1

November 4

Daily Devotion for DESTINY:

Luke 1:28-30 (English Standard Version) - **28** And he came to her and said, "Greetings, O favored one, the Lord is with you!"[a] **29** But she was greatly troubled at the saying, and tried to discern what sort of greeting this might be. **30** And the angel said to her, "Do not be afraid, Mary, for you have found favor with God.

Throughout the Bible, one common theme is repeated when we discover our assignment in life - submission! By now, we should be getting a strong sense of our destiny. Initially, it may be something that we never saw ourselves doing and at this point, do not have a desire to do. If you will just trust God and submit to what God has called you to, you will find that your life will be all that you imagined and more.

Let's look at Mary, the mother of our Lord and Savior, Jesus. During that time, many young women (virgins) were hoping that their destiny would be to bring the promised Messiah into the world. Mary, on the other hand was engaged to Joseph, so when the angel appeared to her to let her know that she had been chosen by God for this very important assignment, she did not initially feel favored. It would mean losing Joseph, but when she submitted to God; He took care of Joseph! Walking out her destiny was no piece of cake, but in the end, she was honored to have been chosen for this unique assignment.

I want to encourage you today to submit to God as He begins to reveal to you the reason for your existence. You may lose many important relationships (family and friends) and you may even have to walk alone, but in the end, it will be life-changing; not only for you, but also those that you have been assigned to!

Luke 1:42; Isaiah 43:5; Judges 6:12

November 5

Daily Devotion for DESTINY:

Psalms 91:9-11 (English Standard Version) - Because you have made the Lord your dwelling place the Most High, who is my refuge **no** evil shall be allowed to befall you, no plague come near your tent. For he will command his angels concerning you to guard you in all your ways.

Good afternoon! As I was in the process of posting the Daily Devotion for today, I saw the terrible news about the church shooting in Sutherland Springs, TX. After praying for the families of the victims, my immediate response is to combat fear.

Please take a moment to read our scripture for today in its entirety. I encourage you to pray this scripture over you, your children and everyone else connected to you on a regular basis.

We are not moved by what we see or feel, we are only moved by the Word of God. The Word of God says that He has given His angels charge over you to keep you in all your ways! Believe that!!!

Psalms 91:1-16; Hebrews 13:6; Deuteronomy 31:6

November 6

Daily Devotion for DESTINY:

Psalms 16:1 (Amplified Bible, classic edition) - **1** Keep *and* protect me, O God, for in You I have found refuge, *and* in You do I put my trust *and* hide myself.

Happy Meditation Day! This week, we are going to focus on the protection that God provides for His children. Our scripture today is a prayer that David prayed committing himself to the protection of God.

To take refuge in God means to trust God without any reservations. This, in turn means that we must submit wholeheartedly to God and hide ourselves in Him.

This week, let's start each day by praying a hedge of protection around not only us, but everyone that is connected to us as we go about our day.

Isaiah 54:17; Exodus 14:14; Psalms 119:114

November 7

Daily Devotion for DESTINY:

I John 2:15-16 (English Standard Version) - **15** Do not love the world or the things in the world. If anyone loves the world, the love of the Father is not in him. **16** For all that is in the world—the desires of the flesh and the desires of the eyes and pride of life[a]—is not from the Father but is from the world.

It is Transformation Day! As children of God, we are not to love the things of the world. The things of the world refer to the pleasures of our flesh. When we are born again, our goal is to transform our minds to love the things of God. When we do this, our flesh will follow.

We cannot love the world and love God at the same time. The love of the world forces out the love of the Father and the love of the Father forces out the love of the world. Choose ye this day!

This year, lets transform our minds to love God and not the world.

Matthew 6:24; Joshua 24:15; Luke 16:13

November 8

Daily Devotion for DESTINY:

James 3:17 (The Amplified Bible, classic edition) - **17** But the wisdom from above is first of all pure (undefiled); then it is peace-loving, courteous (considerate, gentle). [It is willing to] yield to reason, full of compassion and good fruits; it is wholehearted *and straightforward*, impartial *and* unfeigned (free from doubts, wavering, and insincerity).

Happy wisdom Day! By now, we should begin to feel our wisdom increasing. It is the perfect time to do a wisdom check. What this means is that we want to make sure that the wisdom that we are developing is not driven by envy and selfish ambition but is dependent on God.

True wisdom is full of mercy, impartial, sincere and does not pretend to get what it wants out of other people. To sum it up, true wisdom is the ability to live in a manner pleasing to God and applying His wisdom to every area of our lives.

Today (and every day) let's make sure that our wisdom is continually growing according to God's word.

James 1:17; James 1:5; Luke 21:15

November 9

Daily Devotion for DESTINY:

Psalms 100:4 (Amplified Bible, classic edition) - **4** Enter into His gates with thanksgiving *and* a thank offering and into His courts with praise! Be thankful *and* say so to Him, bless *and affectionately* praise His name!

It is Thankful Day and I would like to share a portion of a prayer from Prophetess Tonya S. Hall. I pray that it blesses you as it blessed me.

Father, today we thank you for an understanding in areas that seem unclear. We receive the anointing of abundant wisdom that we can confidently make the right decisions for our destiny. We confess by faith that we dwell in the habitation that God has ordained for our lives. We will not make permanent decisions in temporary situations.

We cover our lives and our family's lives, purpose and destiny in the blood of Jesus. The plans of the enemy will be ineffective. We walk in the grace to avoid excuses instead we accept the responsibility required to maximize the message of reconciliation.

We embrace the mission with vigor to make Jesus FAMOUS! Today is our day of Victory in Jesus' name!!!!

Hebrews 13:15; Psalms 96:2; I Chronicles 29:13

November 10

Daily Devotion for DESTINY:

Galatians 3:21-22 (New Living Translation) - **21** Is there a conflict, then, between God's law and God's promises?[a] Absolutely not! If the law could give us new life, we could be made right with God by obeying it. **22** But the Scriptures declare that we are all prisoners of sin, so we receive God's promise of freedom only by believing in Jesus Christ.

Happy Faith Day! In our scripture today, Paul is addressing whether God's laws are in conflict with God's promises. God is a God of purpose. He gave both the laws and the promises for different purposes. It is inconceivable to think that God conflicts with Himself.

The purpose of the law was to show us how deep in sin we have gone. The purpose of grace (and God's promises) is to save us from the sin that is trying to destroy us. The law cannot cause eternal life. It takes faith in God and His word to receive eternal life.

This year, let's allow God to show us the areas of our lives where we need to go higher. Let's apply our faith to help us in this endeavor.

Romans 8:2-4; Galatians 2:21; Galatians 3:23

November 11

Daily Devotion for DESTINY:

Ephesians 2:10 (The Amplified Bible, classic edition) - **10** For we are God's [own] handiwork (His workmanship), [a]recreated in Christ Jesus, [born anew] that we may do those good works which God predestined (planned beforehand) for us [taking paths which He prepared ahead of time], that we should walk in them [living the good life which He prearranged and made ready for us to live].

Our scripture today tells us who we are in God. We are God's masterpieces. God is working out the plan in our lives that He ordained for us even before we were born.

As we walk through this life, God is teaching us, training us and applying the finishing touches in all of the right places to make us exactly the way He imagined us to be when He created us.

This year, let's submit to the Potter's wheel and allow God's design for us to manifest itself! Let's make our Father proud!!!

Philippians 2:13; Colossians 1:10; Hebrews 13:21

November 12

Daily Devotion for DESTINY:

Isaiah 43:19 (The Amplified Bible, classic edition) - **19** Behold, I am doing a new thing! Now it springs forth; do you not perceive *and* know it *and* will you not give heed to it? I will even make a way in the wilderness and rivers in the desert.

Good morning! I feel that I have addressed this before, but it is heavy on my heart this morning, so maybe there is someone who needs it now. The Prophet Isaiah wrote our scripture today to the children of Israel at a very bad time in their lives. They were in captivity, they had lost everything that they thought they would have by now and they were homesick for the land that God had promised them.

Do you feel like the children of Israel? Has life dealt you a blow that you don't know how to handle? Then don't handle it! Let God handle it by doing a new thing in your life! Change your focus from the past to the present. Don not dwell any longer on what has happened in the past. Even if your past was good, allow God to take your life to the next level and make it great!

This year, let's not dwell on the former things (good or bad). Let's move on to the new thing that God is patiently waiting to give to us!

Isaiah 65:17; Isaiah 42:9; Revelation 21:5

November 13

Daily Devotion for DESTINY:

Psalms 119:11 (New King James Version) - Your word I have hidden in my heart, That I might not sin against You.

Happy Meditation Day! The Psalmist knew the secret to overcoming sin; hiding the word of God in his heart. How do we hide the word of God in our hearts? We meditate on it day and night. Proverbs 4:23 tells us to guard our heats because out of it flows the issues of life.

We think, know, understand and experience emotions from our heart. If we have meditated on God's word until it is in our hearts, any issues we face will be affected by the word that we have hidden.

This year, let's treat God's word like the treasure it is. Let's meditate on it until it is stored so deep in our hearts that we will not be able to sin.

Proverbs 4:23; Psalms 37:31; Jeremiah 15:16

November 14

Daily Devotion for DESTINY:

I Peter 4:12 (New King James Version) - **12** Beloved, do not think it strange concerning the fiery trial which is to try you, as though some strange thing happened to you;

It is Transformation Day! Many of us expect all of our problems to go away once we accept Jesus into our lives. We soon realize that our trials are just beginning. There are many reasons for this, but I just want to address one of the reasons today.

When we are born again, we must transform our thinking so that our bodies line up with our new spirit. This is done by testing our faith through trials and tribulations. The more trials that we come through victoriously, the more transformation that is taking place in us.

James 1:3-4 lets us know that the testing of our faith produces patience and patience produces a life that is complete and lacking nothing. This is the transformed life!

II Timothy 3:12; I Peter 5:9; James 1:3-4

November 15

Daily Devotion for DESTINY:

Matthew 16:24 (English Standard Version) - **24** Then Jesus told his disciples, "If anyone would come after me, let him deny himself and take up his cross and follow me.

It is Wisdom Day! Today, I would like to glean the wisdom out of a very familiar passage of scripture. In our scripture today, Jesus told His disciples that if they want to walk with Him, they must do two things: deny themselves and take up their cross and FOLLOW HIM.

The same goes for us today. Following Jesus means moving on from the place (level) where you accepted Him into your heart into your place of destiny. In other words, we must keep growing once we receive Jesus into our hearts. This journey will require us to take up our cross (make sacrifices) and be willing to deny ourselves to follow Jesus.

For the remainder of this year, lets lose sight of our wants and desires and gain sigh of God's desires for us. Let's follow Jesus to our destiny!

Matthew 10:38; Luke 14:27; Mark 8:34

November 16

Daily Devotion for DESTINY:

Isaiah 43:7 (New King James Version) - Everyone who is called by My name, Whom I have created for My glory; I have formed him, yes, I have made him."

It is Thankful Day! Throughout this year, we have been learning how to discover the reason for our existence and how to carry out that assignment. There is one common purpose that each one of us share. We were created for God's own glory and to glorify God.

What does it mean to glorify God? It means that we bring Him honor in what we think, how we act and what we say. It means to acknowledge God's glory and make His glory known to those who come across our paths.

This year, let's glorify God by developing a thankful heart for everything that He has done for us.

I Corinthians 10:31; Psalms 86:12; Psalms 115:1

November 17

Daily Devotion for DESTINY:

Proverbs 3:4 (The Amplified Bible, classic edition) - **4** So shall you find favor, good understanding, *and* high esteem in the sight [or judgment] of God and man.

Happy Faith Day and we have the favor of God today! It is very important that we realize the favor that God gives His children when we seek to please Him! It takes favor to reach our destiny. We are going to have to walk in faith not only to recognize the doors that God is opening, but to walk through them.

We not only have favor with God, but we also have favor with men. Why? Most of the time, God uses men to open the doors of opportunity for us. That is why Hebrews 13:2 tells us to be careful how we treat strangers because we may be entertaining God's provision (angels) without even knowing it.

This year, let's begin to recognize and walk through the doors that God is opening for us. Once we do, we will have the opportunity to be the tool that God uses to open doors for others.

Hebrews 13:2; Luke 2:52; I Samuel 2:26

November 18

Daily Devotion for DESTINY:

Matthew 7:7 (English Standard Version) - **7** "Ask, and it will be given to you; seek, and you will find; knock, and it will be opened to you.

Today, I would like to talk about what I like to call "Destiny Doors". To summarize, we have learned that the key to opening the door to our destiny is asking God to reveal our destinies to us(prayer).

In addition to asking, we must seek. God rarely reveals our destiny right away or all at once. God tends to show us A and Z in hopes that we will seek Him for the in-between details. This is His way of making sure that we walk by faith knowing and believing that He will direct our paths.

For the remainder of this year, let's ask, seek, knock then walk through our Destiny Doors!

Matthew 21:12; John 15:16; Mark 11:24

November 19

Daily Devotion for DESTINY:

Psalms 139:16 (The Living Bible) - **16** You saw me before I was born and scheduled each day of my life before I began to breathe. Every day was recorded in your book!

God knows everything that will happen in our lives. He knows all of the decisions that we will make (good and bad) and He knows all of the consequences that we reap from our bad decisions.

God laid out the path for our lives (destiny) then gave us the free will to choose whether we desire to follow that path. Why did He give us free will? Because just like humans, He wanted us to choose to please Him even though He has the power to make that decision for us.

This year, let's choose to follow the path that God laid out for us even before we were born!

Psalms 55:8; Malachi 3:16; Revelation 20:12

November 20

Daily Devotion for DESTINY:

Ii Corinthians 5:17 (English Standard Version) - **17** Therefore, if anyone is in Christ, he is a new creation.[a] The old has passed away; behold, the new has come.

Happy Meditation Day! Today, I would like to encourage you to cease meditating on your past and focus on your future. One of the main tools that satan uses against us is guilt. The enemy encourages us to do things that are not pleasing to God, then make us feel guilty for doing them.

Please know that God does not make us feel guilty. God convicts our heart. The way that you tell the difference between guilt and conviction is that guilt feelings leave you with a sense of hopelessness. Conviction gives you hope and the only thing that you want to do is ask God, your Father to forgive you.

Today (and every day) as you meditate on the Word of God, pay close attention to your feelings. If you feel that there is no hope for your situation, rebuke the devil, repent to God for missing the mark and MOVE ON!!!

Ephesians 4:22-24; Psalms 51:10; Romans 8:1

November 21

Daily Devotion for DESTINY:

Ephesians 4:22-24 (English Standard Version) - **22** to put off your old self,[a] which belongs to your former manner of life and is corrupt through deceitful desires, **23** and to be renewed in the spirit of your minds, **24** and to put on the new self, created after the likeness of God in true righteousness and holiness.

It is Transformation Day! Today, I would like to talk about the transformation that a caterpillar goes through to become a butterfly because it is very similar to the transformation that we, as Christians, go through to become the beautiful creation that God had in mind when He made us.

There are many stages to the caterpillar's transformation, but the most notable stage is the beginning stage. The caterpillar eats everything in sight at this stage because the nutrition is what carries him through the transformation. We could learn something from this. We must meditate (constantly chew) on the Word of God to become the butterfly that God created.

Perhaps you have not made it through the transformation because you have not eaten enough of God's word. It is not too late! For the remainder of this year, increase your appetite and eat the Word of God like never before! Become the beautiful creation that God desires for you to be!

Joshua 1:8; romans 6:6; Colossians 3:10

November 22

Daily Devotion for DESTINY:

I Corinthians 1:25 (English Standard Version) - **25** For the foolishness of God is wiser than men, and the weakness of God is stronger than men.

It is Wisdom Day! God's greatest plans are often executed through what man considers weak or even foolish. Many times, that which God appoints, requires and commands is considered to be foolish to man.

In our scripture today, Paul is suggesting that if it were possible (and we know that it is not!) for God to be weak or foolish, His foolishness and weakness would still be much stronger and wiser than our human strength and wisdom.

Now that we have put this into perspective, let's operate in the wisdom of God and not in our own wisdom.

II Corinthians 14:4; II Corinthians 13:4; I Corinthians 1:18

November 23

Daily Devotion for DESTINY:

Psalms 30:12(The Amplified Bible, classic edition) - **12** To the end that my tongue *and* my heart *and* everything glorious within me may sing praise to You and not be silent. O Lord my God, I will give thanks to You forever.

Happy Thankful Day! In our scripture today, David had many great reasons to praise the Lord. God had kept him alive and healthy. God had delivered him from death and from the hand of his enemies.

Sometimes in life, we need to drop everything that keeps us so busy each day and give thanks to our God. At this point in our scripture, God had transformed David's mourning into dancing.

We are called to live with a grateful heart every day, not just on Thanksgiving. This year, let's develop an attitude of gratitude and watch God work in our lives!

Psalms 146:1-2; Luke 19:40; Psalms 16:9

November 24

Daily Devotion for DESTINY:

James 1:6 (The Amplified Bible, classic edition) -**6** Only it must be in faith that he asks with no wavering (no hesitating, no doubting). For the one who wavers (hesitates, doubts) is like the billowing surge out at sea that is blown hither *and* thither and tossed by the wind.

Happy favor-filled Faith Day! We cannot hope to obtain any favor from God if we do not walk in faith. Where there is no faith, we will lack the wisdom necessary to guide us into our destiny.

In some cases, we may not be sure that what we are asking God for is His will for our lives. In these cases, we cannot come to Him with unwavering faith, but we can come to Him with unwavering confidence knowing that if what we ask is for our good and in His will, He will do it for us.

This year, let's continue to seek the mind of Christ so that we can have unwavering faith and know that what we are believing God for is His perfect will for our lives.

Ephesians 4:14; Hebrews 10:23; Hebrews 13:9

November 25

Daily Devotion for DESTINY:

Psalms 138:8 (The Amplified Bible, classic edition) - **8** The Lord will perfect that which concerns me; Your mercy *and* loving-kindness, O Lord, endure forever—forsake not the works of Your own hands.

As believing children of God, our confession is that our lives are unfolding the will of God. Our scripture today makes a bold assertion of faith that the Lord will perfect (bring to completion) His will for our lives.

The Lord instilled a knowing in my spirit many years ago that if something concerns me (no matter how big or how small), it concerns God and His is working it out. What are you concerned about today? Your children, your health, your finances?

This year, allow God to perfect those things and concern you and rest in Him!

Philippians 1:6; Psalms 57:2; I Thessalonians 5:24

November 26

Daily Devotion for DESTINY:

John 15:15 (The Amplified Bible, classic edition) - **15** I do not call you servants (slaves) any longer, for the servant does not know what his master is doing (working out). But I have called you My friends, because I have made known to you everything that I have heard from My Father. [I have revealed to you everything that I have learned from Him.]

Good morning! Most theologians agree that our scripture today was Jesus talking to His disciples at the close of the last supper which was the night that He was betrayed. It is interesting to me what Jesus chose to talk about in His last hours on this earth....Friendship!

Jesus considers us as believers to be His friends. What an honor! I talked earlier about divine connections. This is the most important connection we should have. Jesus has revealed to us everything that He heard and learned from our Father God. Because of this, we have everything we need to successfully fulfill our destiny.

If you need a friend today, I recommend Jesus!

Psalms 25:14; Matthew 13:11; Ephesians 1:9

November 27

Daily Devotion for DESTINY:

Philippians 4:8 (The Amplified Bible, classic edition) - **8** For the rest, brethren, whatever is true, whatever is worthy of reverence *and* is honorable *and* seemly, whatever is just, whatever is pure, whatever is lovely *and* lovable, whatever is kind *and* winsome *and gracious*, if there is any virtue *and* excellence, if there is anything worthy of praise, think on *and* weigh *and* take account of these things [fix your minds on them].

It is Meditation Day! Today, I just want to reiterate the things that we should be meditating on. The enemy does not mind you meditating as long as you are not meditating on anything that will enhance your spiritual growth.

Our scripture today spells out for us the things that will cause us to grow spiritually if we meditate on them. These things can be found in the Word of God.

For the remainder of the year, let's make sure that we are meditating on those things which are true, honorable, just, pure, lovely commendable, excellent and worthy of praise as we advance towards our destiny.

Joshua 1:8; Psalms 1:2; Psalms 104:34

November 28

Daily Devotion for DESTINY:

II Corinthians 5:17 (English Standard Version) - **17** Therefore, if anyone is in Christ, he is a new creation.[a] The old has passed away; behold, the new has come.

It is Transformation Day! Some people may be wondering why Romans 12:2 instructs Christians to transform (renew) our minds and why I am dedicating one day a week to this subject if all things became new when we accepted Jesus as Lord and Savior of our lives.

Here is why: We are a three-part being; spirit, soul & body. When we are born again, Our SPIRIT (only) is renewed. We must transform our souls (mind, will & emotions) so that our bodies will now live according to our new spirit. We do this by reading (meditating) the Word of God so that we will begin to think like Him. When our minds are transformed, our bodies will follow.

This year, let's make sure that our soul and body lines up with the Word of God.

Romans 12:2; Psalms 51:10; Ezekiel 11:19

November 29

Daily Devotion for DESTINY:

Proverbs 8:33 (The Amplified Bible, classic edition) - **33** Hear instruction and be wise, and do not refuse *or* neglect it.

It is Wisdom Day! We have learned that the source of Godly wisdom is the bible. There is not a question you will have or a circumstance that you will face that the answer cannot be found in God's word. God's principles are relevant to every situation and decision that we will encounter.

Just to clarify: Knowledge is information; understanding is the capacity to comprehend knowledge and wisdom is the ability to apply knowledge. We acquire wisdom gradually as we hide God's word in our hearts.

This year, let's expand our capacity to see things from the Lord's point of view so that we will respond according to biblical principles.

Proverbs 4:1; Proverbs 5:1; Proverbs 1:8

November 30

Daily Devotion for DESTINY:

I Thessalonians 5:16-18 (English Standard Version) - **6** Rejoice always, **17** pray without ceasing, **18** give thanks in all circumstances; for this is the will of God in Christ Jesus for you.

It is Thankful Day! As believers, there are some things that should always be a part of our lives and actions. Our scripture today talks about three of the things. We should always rejoice, always pray and always be thankful.

What does it mean to rejoice? Rejoice is a Christian concept that refers to an inward emotion that has an outward expression. What does it mean to pray? Prayer is a **Two-way** communication between you and God. We not only talk to Him, but we also listen when He talks to us.

This year, let's make it a goal to be always joyful, always thankful and always prayerful!

Psalms 40:16; Psalms 5:11; Philippians 4:4

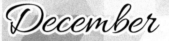

December

²⁸ And we know that in all things God works
for the good of those who love him,
who^[a] have been called according to his purpose.

Romans 8:28 (NIV)

December 1

Daily Devotion for DESTINY:

Romans 8:28 (The Amplified Bible, classic edition) - **28** We are assured *and* know that [[a]God being a partner in their labor] all things work together *and* are [fitting into a plan] for good to *and* for those who love God and are called according to [His] design *and purpose.*

Happy Faith Day! Our scripture today is one that I would like for you to focus on and apply your faith to. Believe today that ALL things are working together for your good. Yes, even that thing! In the midst of whatever you are going through. If you believe that God has your best interest at heart; it is working together for your good.

The fact that you are still in the fight proves that God is not finished yet. He is creating solutions, strategies and blessings right now to bring you out victoriously! Go is fighting with and for you! Believe that!

This year, be at peace and know that with God fighting for you, your enemy is outnumbered!

I Peter 5:10; James 1:12; Genesis 50:12

December 2

Daily Devotion for DESTINY:

Luke 21:17 (The Amplified Bible, classic edition) - **17** And you will be hated (despised) by everyone because [you bear] My name *and* for its sake.

Now that God is beginning to reveal our destiny and purpose to us, I think that it is very important that you understand that not everyone is going to celebrate the call of God on your life.

They will look at the favor of God on you, the doors that He is opening for you, the divine connections that He arranged for you and instead of seeing your potential and being happy for you, they will only see what they don't have and what they have not achieved.

This year, do not allow their negativity to affect you. Pray for them, believe God is working on them and KEEP IT MOVING!

I Peter 5:8; John 15:18; Psalms 41:11-12

December 3

Daily Devotion for DESTINY:

Ecclesiastes 3:1 (The Amplified Bible, classic edition) - **3** To everything there is a season, and a time for every matter *or purpose* under heaven:

We are in a season of growth. I have dedicated to growing in the areas of meditation, transformation, wisdom, praise and faith. This was in preparation for the upcoming year.

Many of us will be entering into a season of destiny in 2018. We will make more progress in 2018 than we have made in the past several years! All of the strength that we have developed this year will be put to use in 2018.

For the remainder of this year, our declaration is that God is going to supernaturally provide everything we need to fulfill our destiny!

Proverbs 15:23; Ecclesiastes 7:14; Ecclesiastes 3:18

December 4

Daily Devotion for DESTINY:

Psalms 1:1-3 (The Amplified Bible, classic edition) - **1** Blessed (happy, fortunate, prosperous, and enviable) is the man who walks *and* lives not in the counsel of the unGodly [following their advice, their plans and purposes], nor stands [submissive and inactive] in the path where sinners walk, nor sits down [to relax and rest] where the scornful [and the mockers] gather. **2** But his delight *and* desire are in the law of the Lord, and on His law (the precepts, the instructions, the teachings of God) he habitually meditates (ponders and studies) by day and by night. **3** And he shall be like a tree firmly planted [and tended] by the streams of water, ready to bring forth its fruit in its season; its leaf also shall not fade *or* wither; and everything he does shall prosper [and come to maturity].

Happy Meditation Day! Our scripture today is a beatitude. In Matthew 5:3-11, we see more beatitudes that Jesus taught in His sermon on the Mount. A beatitude pronounces conditional blessings on a certain group of people.

This beatitude lets us know that we are blessed when we do not go along with or follow the actions of the wicked (Those who do not agree with God's way of thinking). As Christians, our delight is in meditating on the word of God and applying it to our lives.

This year, let's not stand in the path of sinners by our conduct, but let our words and actions lead the sinner to our God!

Proverbs 4:14-15; Psalms 119:11; Jeremiah 17:8

December 5

Daily Devotion for DESTINY:

Romans 12:2 (The Amplified Bible, classic edition) - **2** Do not be conformed to this world (this age), [fashioned after and adapted to its external, superficial customs], but be transformed (changed) by the [entire] renewal of your mind [by its new ideals and its new attitude], so that you may prove [for yourselves] what is the good and acceptable and perfect will of God, *even* the thing which is good and acceptable and perfect [in His sight for you].

It is Transformation Day! We have looked at this scripture before, but I wanted to dig a little deeper. What does the bible mean when it says, "Don not be conformed to this world"?

Satan has created an atmosphere in this world that leads people away from God and into sin. We, as Christians are not to fit (conform) into the mold (pattern) of this world (atmosphere) The Christian will lead our brothers and sisters out of sin and to our God.

This year, let's not conform to the atmosphere that satan has created. Let's change the atmosphere to what God intended it to be!

I Peter 1:14; II Corinthians 6:18; I John 2:15-17

December 6

Daily Devotion for DESTINY:

Proverbs 2:6 (The Amplified Bible, classic edition) - **6** For the Lord gives skillful *and* Godly Wisdom; from His mouth come knowledge and understanding.

It is Wisdom Day! A gentleman named Robert Short gave his opinion of the world's situation today and I have to say that I agree wholeheartedly. He stated "The situation today is: lots of knowledge, but little understanding. Lots of means, but little meaning. Lots of know-how, but little know-why. Lots of sight, but little insight.

The bottom line is that the thing that we are lacking most today is wisdom. Our goal this year has been to change that perception; one person at a time, beginning with us.

This year, lets continue to seek the wisdom of God and live the life that He desires for us.

James 1:5; I Kings 3:12; James 1:17

December 7

Daily Devotion for DESTINY:

I Thessalonians 5:18 (The Amplified Bible, classic edition) – **18** Thank [God] in everything [no matter what the circumstances may be, be thankful and give thanks], for this is the will of God for you [who are] in Christ Jesus [the Revealer and Mediator of that will].

It is Thankful Day! Being thankful to God is more than just words. An attitude (lifestyle) of thanksgiving in both tribulations and blessings is what distinguishes the Christian from everyone else. Being thankful is a very good start to walking in the will of God for our lives.

On the other hand, being ungrateful hinders the hand of God. If we have children or have been around children that displayed ungratefulness, I am sure that you would agree that make you hesitant to give or do anything for them. So it is with our Father.

This year, lets untie the hand of God by living the lifestyle of thankfulness and allowing Him to bless us as He so desires.

Ephesians 5:20; romans 5:3-5; Romans 1:21

December 8

Daily Devotion for DESTINY:

I Samuel 26:23 (English Standard Version) - **23** The Lord rewards every man for his righteousness and his faithfulness, for the Lord gave you into my hand today, and I would not put out my hand against the Lord's anointed.

Happy Faith Day! It has been a year of preparation for those of us who are determined to walk out our destiny. We must do what we have been called to do speedily because we are preparing for the return of the King!

God wants to position, prosper and heal His people so that we can carry out the assignment that He has given to us. Anything that we receive from God in this very crucial hour is directly proportionate to our level of righteousness and our level of faith; therefore, we must focus on building our faith!

The Lord rewards the righteous and the faithful. This year, lets focus on building our faith so that we can walk out our destiny!

Psalms 62:12; Nehemiah 13:14; I Kings 8:32

December 9

Daily Devotion for DESTINY

I Peter 1:13 (English Standard Version) - **13** Therefore, preparing your minds for action,[a] and being sober-minded, set your hope fully on the grace that will be brought to you at the revelation of Jesus Christ.

If we don't understand our battle, we will not win it. Our battle in this season is mainly with our own selves. Yes, it is true that satan has sent his imps to distract us because his goal is to take our minds off the battle that is going on within us.

We are on a path in life where God is not just interested in us doing what He has called us to do, but He is also interested in us becoming who He has called us to be. If we become who God called us to be, we will automatically do what He has called us to do. The struggle comes when we try to do it before we become it.

For the remainder of this year, lets focus on becoming who God has called us to be and everything else will fall into place.

I Peter 4:7; I Peter 5:8; II Timothy 4:5

December 10

Daily Devotion for DESTINY:

Mark 1:15 (The Amplified Bible, classic edition) - **15** And saying, The [appointed period of] time is fulfilled (completed), and the kingdom of God is at hand; repent ([a]have a change of mind which issues in regret for past sins and in change of conduct for the better) and believe (trust in, rely on, and adhere to) the good news (the Gospel).

We are in a period of divine acceleration. What is divine acceleration? It is the supernatural ability of God applied to our destiny to bring it to pass at a much faster rate than humanly possible. There are people, communities, jobs, churches, etc. waiting on you to get there.

God is now ready to use us. Many of us have spent this year getting rid of our own agenda, so now God is ready to use us to carry out His agenda. Many of us are coming into a Kairos moment. Kairos is a period of time where everything comes together for you to have a supernatural experience. A Kairos moment is orchestrated by God.

This year, the conditions are right for a Kairos moment for many of us. God is assigning Angels to go ahead of us to set up our Kairos moment. Do not miss your moment!

Ephesians 1:10; Galatians 4:4; Luke 10:11

December 11

Daily Devotion for DESTINY:

Deuteronomy 28:2 (The Amplified Bible, classic edition) - **2** And all these blessings shall come upon you and overtake you if you heed the voice of the Lord your God.

Happy Meditation Day! Today, I would like to talk about the unusual circumstances that occurred a few days ago. I am speaking about all of the snow that fell in unusual places such as Texas, Mississippi, Georgia and Florida.

As I was looking at pictures and videos of the snowfall in these places, I could hear God speaking to my spirit to expect the unexpected. Yes, we will begin to see those things that we have been expecting, but in this season; we are going to begin to see things that we have not been expecting.

This has been a year of preparation for us, now sit back, relax and allow God's unexpected blessings to overtake you!

Isaiah 1:19; Haggai 2:19; Genesis 26:12

December 12

Daily Devotion for DESTINY:

Ii Corinthians 5:17 (The Amplified Bible, classic edition) - **17** Therefore if any person is [engrafted] in Christ (the Messiah) he is a new creation (a new creature altogether); the old [previous moral and spiritual condition] has passed away. Behold, the fresh *and* new has come!

It is Transformation Day! Our minds were made to change. They were never meant to stay the same. God intended for our minds to continually develop and mature.

There are some new things coming in this season that will require a transformed mind. If you do not transform your mind, you will not experience the new thing. Many people are defeated in this fight because they cannot win the battle in their own mind.

God always checks our transformation before He takes us to a new level. This year, let's make sure that we have grown from where we were this time last year. Let's show God that we can handle the new level that He is taking us to!

Ezekiel 36:26; John 3:3; Psalms 51:10

December 13

Daily Devotion for DESTINY:

Daniel 2:21 (The Amplified Bible, classic edition) - **21** He changes the times and the seasons; He removes kings and sets up kings. He gives wisdom to the wise and knowledge to those who have understanding!

It is Wisdom Day! Our scripture today was written by Daniel while he was in captivity in Babylon. Even in captivity, Daniel help prominent positions because he understood that God is the source of all wisdom and knowledge; therefore, he walked in wisdom.

God formed each of our intellect and made it what it is today. Daniel contributes that to God what some people attribute to nature and to chance. Daniel was thankful to God for the wisdom He gave him during his 70 years of captivity.

God has placed each one of us on this earth with a distinct purpose in the development of His great plans. Let us continue to discover His plan and walk therein.

Proverbs 2:6-7; James 1:5; I Kings 4:29

December 14

Daily Devotion for DESTINY:

Psalms 107:1 (The Amplified Bible, classic edition) - **1** O give thanks to the Lord, for He is good; for His mercy *and* loving-kindness endure forever!

Welcome to Thankful Day! One of the most important qualities that we can develop as Christians is thankfulness. We learned last week that we are to give thanks IN every situation, not FOR every situation. There is a difference.

Pastor Tony Evans said that God is the entity that is most taken for granted in all of the universe. I totally agree! Sometimes we act as though God owes us something and not the other way around.

I encourage you this year to let God know that we do not take Him for granted, but we are dependent on Him and thankful to Him for everything that He has done, is doing and will do for us!

I Thessalonians 5:18; Psalms 92:1; Psalms 100:4

December 15

Daily Devotion for DESTINY:

Deuteronomy 29:29 (The Amplified Bible, classic edition) - **29** The secret things belong unto the Lord our God, but the things which are revealed belong to us and to our children forever, that we may do all of the words of this law.

Happy Faith Day! Bishop T.D. Jakes taught us that faith is not an experience, it is a journey. It is a crucial part of our journey towards our destiny. He went on to say that this faith journey will take us from speculation to revelation.

In other words, we will not be sitting around watching for something to happen and operating in theories with no evidence, but we will now operate in the divine supernatural knowledge of God that He has revealed to us.

This year, let believe God to reveal His will to us and begin walking in revelation towards our destiny!

Amos 3:7; I Corinthians 2:10; Proverbs 25:2

December 16

Daily Devotion for DEESTINY:

Proverbs 4:25 (The Amplified Bible, classic edition) - **25** Let your eyes look right on [with fixed purpose], and let your gaze be straight before you.

I woke up this morning hearing this song in my spirit:

I'm not going back, I'm moving ahead

I'm here to declare to you the past is over in you

All things are made new, surrendered my life to Christ

I'm moving forward!!

You make all things new, yes you make all things new

And I will follow you forward!!

This is the time of year when satan focuses on trying to convince us that the things that we have been focusing on all year has not worked. Please know that this is a lie from the pits of hell.

You have made tremendous progress this year in your journey towards your destiny and I encourage you to continue moving forward with God!!!

Proverbs 3:5-6; Psalms 32:8;Isaiah 43:18

December 17

Daily Devotion for DESTINY:

Ephesians 2:10 (English Standard Version) - **10** For we are his workmanship, created in Christ Jesus for good works, which God prepared beforehand, that we should walk in them.

I am amazed at the amount of people (family & friends) that do not believe that God gave them a specific assignment in life. They feel that the only thing that God requires of them is to accept Jesus into their hearts.

Make no mistake about it, that is way better than the alternative, but please know that we are saved to save others. The purpose of our specific assignments is to build the Kingdom of God.

Settle in your mind this year that you will find our destiny and fulfill it. There is someone out there waiting on you to do just that!

Jeremiah 29:11; Luke 14:23; Jeremiah 1:5

December 18

Daily Devotion for DESTINY:

Philippians 4:8 (English Standard Version) - **8** Finally, brothers, whatever is true, whatever is honorable, whatever is just, whatever is pure, whatever is lovely, whatever is commendable, if there is any excellence, if there is anything worthy of praise, think about these things.

Happy Meditation Day! We are at the very end of the year and I would like to end our Mediation Days with the same scripture that I began them with. This scripture spells out for us the things that we as Christians should meditate on.

It is very important that we realize that meditation is one of the ways that we open our spirits up to receive. While our spirits are open, be careful to only receive the things into our spirits that will glorify God.

This year and all of the years to come, let's make sure that we set aside time to meditate and reflect on God and His goodness towards us. Let this be the focus of our meditation.

Proverbs 4:20-22; Psalms 119:97; Isaiah 26:3

December 19

Daily Devotion for DESTINY:

Romans 12:2 (English Standard Version) - **2** Do not be conformed to this world,[a] but be transformed by the renewal of your mind, that by testing you may discern what is the will of God, what is good and acceptable and perfect.

It is Transformation Day! We began our Transformation days with our scripture for today. As this year draw to a close, I think that it is important to measure our progress.

Looking back over the year, do you feel that your mind has changed? Do you have a better understanding of the bible than you had at the beginning of the year? Do you think more like Christ than you did 6 months ago? Are you on our path towards your destiny?

These are just some of the questions that I am asking myself. If you are able to answer yes to even just one of those questions, you are on the right track! Keep moving forward!

II Corinthians 5:17; Psalms 51:10; Ephesians 4:29

December 20

Daily Devotion for DESTINY:

James 3:17 (English Standard Version) - **17** But the wisdom from above is first pure, then peaceable, gentle, open to reason, full of mercy and good fruits, impartial and sincere.

It is Wisdom Day! Once again, we are circling back around to the true meaning of wisdom. When you set out on a journey, it is important to take time our every so often to assess your progress and determine what (if anything) you should do to make sure you arrive at your destination ON TIME.

In case there is any doubt, my assignment this year has been to let everyone who will listen know that you have been born to fulfill a specific purpose on this earth and give you some of the tools that will help you not only discover your purpose, but also to walk in it.

One very important tool is wisdom. Have we grown in Godly wisdom in ? Ponder on that thought.

James 1:5; Proverbs 12:15; Proverbs 18:15

December 21

Daily Devotion for DESTINY:

Philippians 1:6 (English Standard Version) - **6** And I am sure of this, that he who began a good work in you will bring it to completion at the day of Jesus Christ.

Welcome to Thankful Day! What are you thankful for today? I am thankful that He (God) that has begun a good work in me will continue right up until the time that I see Him face to face.

If you love Jesus and have a heart to please Him, that is something to be thankful for and should not be taken for granted. So many people today do not have the desire to live for God. I am thankful that God chose me to show His love TO and THROUGH so that others will develop the desire to live for Him too.

If you are a recipient of God's love and grace, lets show that love and grace to our brothers and sisters.

Isaiah 63:7; Psalms 126:3; Galatians 2:20

December 22

Daily Devotion for DESTINY:

John 11:14-15 (English Standard Version) - **14** Then Jesus told them plainly, "Lazarus has died, **15** and for your sake I am glad that I was not there, so that you may believe. But let us go to him."

Happy Faith Day! Over the past few weeks, I have heard and/or read several messages on the death AND resurrection of Lazarus. When this happens, I know that there is something that the Lord wants to reveal to me in these messages. Over the next few days, I want to share just a couple of things that the Lord taught me about faith through Lazarus' experience.

The first point is sometimes while we are waiting on God, stuff dies. Now, I am not speaking of the bad things in us that needs to die, but some things that we need die as well. I have always wondered why Jesus waited four days to go and see about his friend, Lazarus. A few days ago, Derick Faizon answered this question for me.

During this time, it was believed that your spirit hovered around your body for three days after you died and could enter back into your body at any moment during those three days. Jesus waited four days so that there would be no doubt that GOD raised Lazarus from the dead!

This year, lets allow God to resurrect our love, joy, peace, wisdom and everything else that has died in your life and should not have. You are going to need these things for the journey that lies ahead.

II Corinthians 4:15; John 12:30; John 11:35-36

December 23

Daily Devotion for Destiny:

John 11:5 (English Standard Version) - **2** It was Mary who anointed the Lord with ointment and wiped his feet with her hair, whose brother Lazarus was ill.

Today, I would like to continue sharing a few points about Lazarus' resurrection.

The second thing that I learned from this experience is that it is very important to have a relationship with Jesus BEFORE things begin to go wrong. Lazarus and his sisters (Mary and Martha) had a special friendship with Jesus before the illness that led to Lazarus' death.

Many people try to operate in faith, but do not have a relationship with God. The only time they come to Him is when they are having a crisis. Because of God's grace, many times He comes to the rescue anyway. He does this in hopes that we will want to build a relationship with Him.

As this year draws to a close, ask yourself if your faith is built on your relationship with God. If you cannot answer a resounding yes to this question, you must make that your first priority as we enter into the new year!

Luke 10:38; John 11:3; 11:35

December 24

Daily Devotion for DESTINY

John 3:16 (The Amplified Bible, classic edition) - **16** For God so greatly loved *and* dearly prized the world that He [even] gave up His only begotten ([a]unique) Son, so that whoever believes in (trusts in, clings to, relies on) Him shall not perish (come to destruction, be lost) but have eternal (everlasting) life.

Happy Christmas Eve! This is the eve that we have chosen to celebrate the greatest gift that God could give to us; His only begotten son, Jesus! We celebrate by giving gifts to our loved ones and our friends.

In the spirit of the season, I am going to spend the remainder of this year discussing the gifts that God put into us before we were born. God instilled in each and every one of us the gifts that we need to fulfill our destiny here on earth.

My hope is that we will add our gifts to everything else that we have discovered this entire year about our destiny. Throughout the year of, we learned that we were born for a specific reason, God has given us a specific assignment and a specific destiny that we must fulfill.

For the remainder of the year as we look at the gifts that God has given his children, let's think about the ones that He has given to us as individuals. We will need them as we step into our destiny!

Romans 5:8; Romans 8:32; I John 4:19

December 25

Daily Devotion for DESTINY:

I Corinthians 12:8 (New King James Version) - **8(a)** for to one is given the word of wisdom;

Merry Christmas! For the remainder of this year, I would like to talk about the spiritual gifts that God has given His children. My hope is that as I talk about these gifts, you will discover which one (s) that God has instilled in you, then allow God to stir them up as you walk towards your destiny. The gifts of the Spirit can be found in I Corinthians 12:8-10. The gifts that God has instilled in you is specific to your destiny.

The first spiritual gift is the word of wisdom. It is considered one of the Revelatory gifts. That is, it is one of the gifts that reveal the mind of God for your life. The word of wisdom is often confused with the word of knowledge; however, they are two very different gifts. The gift of the word of wisdom speaks to the future. It is the ability to speak to things that will come to pass in the future.

Could the Word of Wisdom be one of your Spiritual Gifts?

I Corinthians 2:8; II Corinthians 1:12; II Corinthians 8:7

December 26

Daily Devotion for DESTINY:

I Corinthians 12:8 (New King James Version) - 8(b) to another the word of knowledge through the same Spirit,

We are continuing to look at the Gifts of the Spirit to determine which ones the Lord instilled in us as we continue our walk towards our destiny. Today, we will look at the gift of the Word of Knowledge. This is also considered a Revelatory gift and is often confused with the Gift of Wisdom.

The Gift of the Word of Knowledge is Supernatural ability to know facts about a person, place, time or an event without natural knowledge. Supernatural disclosure of facts as revealed by the Holy Ghost. It is a supernatural release of facts by the Holy Ghost to a vessel.

Could this be one of your Spiritual Gifts?

Romans 15;14; II Corinthians 2:14; II Corinthians 4:6

December 27

Daily Devotion for DESTINY:

I Corinthians 12:9 (a) (New King James Version) - **9** to another faith by the same Spirit,

At this point, I think that it is important to explain the following to help us understand how our gifts are categorized: there are nine gifts of the Spirit that are separated into three categories. The vocal gifts are: the gift of tongues; interpretation of tongues; the gifts of prophecy. The power gifts are: the gift of faith; the working of miracles; gifts of healing. The revelatory gifts are the gifts of word of wisdom; the word of knowledge; the gift of discerning of spirits.

Our Spiritual Gift today is the Gift of Faith. This gift is categorized as one of the Power gifts. Everyone was given a measure (level) of faith, but there are some people who move in a supernatural ability to produce results without toil because of their faith. It is second nature for them to believe God without even thinking about it until the tangible manifestation reaches the earth.

Could this be one of your Spiritual Gifts?

II Corinthians 4:13; Hebrews 11:1; Romans 1:12

December 28

Daily Devotion for DESTINY:

I Corinthians 12:9 (b) (New King James Version) - to another gifts of healings by the same[a] Spirit,

It is Thankful Day! Today, we are going to talk about the Gifts of Healing; not to be confused with the gift of Working of Miracles that we will discuss tomorrow. This gift is also categorized as one of the Power gifts. This is the only gift of the Spirit that is plural in nature.

This gift is plural in nature because when you flow in the gifts of healing, it has the ability to touch any ailment in any realm that affects the human condition: physical, sexual, racial, intellectual, emotionally, etc.

Could this be one of your Spiritual gifts?

I Corinthians 12:28; I Corinthians 12:30; Mark 16:17

December 29,

Daily Devotion for DESTINY:

I Corinthians 12:10 (New King James Version) - **10** to another the working of miracles,

Today, I will like to talk about another Power gift and that is the Working of Miracles. As I stated yesterday, this is often confused with the gifts healing. A gift to reverse the occurrence of natural events. Have authority of the progression of an event that should happen. These miracles speak to the Lordship of Jesus because they show the sovereignty of Jesus by defying all odds in any given situation.

I would just like to include that even though God gets pleasure in performing miracles in our lives, His perfect will is that we live a prosperous (healthy, wealthy, happy) life each and every day! When we are able to be victorious each and every day, there is less need for miracles, which are a temporary fix to our issues. For instance, when we are able to pay our mortgage each month, God does not have to give us a miracle each month to get our mortgage paid.

Could the gift of working of miracles be one of your gifts?

Jeremiah 32:27; John 2:11; Acts 9:11-12

December 30

Daily Devotion for DESTINY:

I Corinthians 12:10 (New King James Version) - **10** to another prophecy, to another *different* kinds of tongues, to another the interpretation of tongues.

Today I want to talk about what is categorized as the Vocal gifts. They are, the Gift of Prophecy, The gift of divers kinds of tongues, The gift of Interpretation of tongues. The following is a summary of these gifts:

Gift of Tongues – This is different that the tongues that you speak because you have the Holy Ghost and the gift of tongues. When you receive the baptism of the Holy Ghost, the immediate sign is speaking in tongues. The bible speaks about other tongues and unknown tongues. Every believer should have a prayer language, but every believer does not have the gift of tongues. The gift of tongues is the supernatural ability from God to deliver a message to a body of people in your heavenly language. It is prophetic in nature; therefore, it must be interpreted.

Interpretation of Tongues- You can have the gift of tongues and not have the interpretation of tongues. Interpretation and translation is not the same thing. You may not know word for word (translate) what the Spirit is saying, but you have a generalized summary of the message (Interpretation) that God wants to convey to His people.

Gift of Prophecy- The articulation of the thoughts, deeds, plans of Heaven. You have the ability to translate the thoughts of God into a known language that the individual understands. If you are filled with the Holy Ghost, you should be able to prophecy.

Could any (or all) of these be your Spiritual gifts?

Luke 2:25-35; Acts 2:1-12; Daniel 5

December 31

Daily Devotion for DESTINY:

I Corinthians 12:10 (New King James Version) - to another discerning of spirits,

Happy New Year's Eve! My goal for these devotions is that you will become aware that God created you for a specific purpose and gave you a specific assignment to fulfill while you are on earth that will build His Kingdom. My hopes are that I have given you the tools that you need to not only discover your purpose, but to complete it all the way to your destination. As you continue in the habit of daily devotions that we have established this year, I have no doubt that each and every one of us will reach our goal.

On this last day of the year, I would like to talk about the last vocal spiritual gift that God has given us. It is the gift of discerning of spirits. The gift of discerning of spirits is the ability to differentiate, define, detect whether invisible activities are Godly, angelic, demonic or fleshly in nature. You will have an insight into what motivates an action. This (as well as the rest) are all gifts that are very valuable to the Kingdom.

Could this be one of your gifts?

I John 4:1; I Thessalonians 5:21; I Corinthians 2:11

CPSIA information can be obtained
at www.ICGtesting.com
Printed in the USA
BVHW031453280219
541446BV00001B/8/P